Cat
Women

Alice Maddicott

Cat
Women

**An Exploration of Feline Friendships
and Lingering Superstitions**

10 9 8 7 6 5 4 3 2 1

First published in 2020 by September Publishing

Copyright © Alice Maddicott 2020

The photos on page 6 and 144 are the author's own.
Other photos are orphan images, sold in shops and online
without any copyright or subject details. If you have any
information about them, please contact the publishers
direct on info@septemberpublishing.org.

The right of Alice Maddicott to be identified as the
author of this work has been asserted by her in accordance
with the Copyright Designs and Patents Act 1988.

Design by April

Fabric on cover: Handtryck, KATTOR by Vicke
Lindstrand © DACS 2020. Photo from Greta Lindström/
Nationalmuseum.

Printed in Poland on paper from responsibly managed,
sustainable sources by L&C Printing Group

ISBN 978-1-912836-06-2

September Publishing
www.septemberpublishing.org

In Loving Memory of Dylan and Hazel Granny

Introduction

I I became a Cat Woman the moment I was hit with a thud of love that I'd never realised a creature could produce. I've always loved animals – as a child I attempted to befriend snails and tried to tame mice so they would sit in my pockets. I took my tortoise to school and I even spent hours up to my knees in my local river trying to tickle trout in the hope that one day they would swim behind me like a train of fishy ribbons, in my very own rural Somerset version of swimming with dolphins.

But one day, when I was in my early thirties, following a sudden move that had left me somewhat adrift, I met a cat who changed my life forever. Or rather, I re-met . . .

Dylan was the Cornish village cat I had seen on holidays for years and always admired from afar – I snuck a stroke whenever I could. But now I was living in his little seaside village where I knew no one except relatives. One day, when out walking, I paused by the large flowerpot in which he was sleeping and gave him a stroke, at which point he stretched and climbed down. After a few minutes I turned to walk back up the street to my house and he followed me home. He came in and curled up on my lap.

It got to night time and I wasn't sure what to do. I had to send him home – I couldn't steal a cat – but there was something about him being there that just made everything feel better. I eventually and very reluctantly turned him out.

But the next morning, when I opened the front door, there he was. He trotted in as if he owned the place and wouldn't budge all day. Night fell and again I turned him out. But each day he came back. I had been thinking of getting a kitten, but now that was impossible. I did not want another cat. I wanted him.

Although in theory he belonged to someone else, each day he would show up and, before long, it was quite obvious that he had decided to move in. I had been a bit of a wreck, but for some reason this beautiful, old, giant tabby cat had chosen me. Soon I belonged to him as much as him to me.

Days turned to weeks, then months, then years. (I hasten to add at this point that his old owners now knew where he was – do not ever actually steal a cat!) The bond sometimes overwhelmed me. He would sit curled up on my lap, sometimes wrap his arms around me as if cuddling, and usually spent the night stretched out down my back. If I went out for a walk he would follow me. He would come to the beach and sniff the seaweed curiously. If I ever bumped into him out and about he would jump up excitedly as if overwhelmed with the adventure of me suddenly appearing.

Those of you who have read Philip Pullman's *His Dark Materials* trilogy will understand when I say that he felt like my daemon – a part of me somehow that it hurt to be away from for too long. We could communicate. If I was feeling ill he would sense the sore spot and curl up on it. If I was sad, he wouldn't leave my side.

Dylan was also a well-known character in the village. I would occasionally hear about his trips to the pub, or how he had been 'helping' at the post office by sitting on the counter. Come summer when the tourists arrived, he couldn't resist sitting outside to be admired (he was very beautiful). But woe betide any dogs who got too close – fluffing up his fur and growling before chasing them away was one of his favourite hobbies.

I guess you could see his kindness and his sensing of when things weren't right as a little uncanny, but how this bond between human and animal, between woman and cat, could be seen as anything but positive is a mystery to me. I felt honoured.

In 2011, partly inspired by my experience with Dylan over the previous year, I began to collect photos of women or girls and their cats. Every time I came across one in a charity shop, junk shop, market or online auction site, I would buy it. It was a strange impulse. Perhaps something akin to the urge to take in a lost cat.

I have always been interested in 'found photos'; I feel a keen poignancy in these images of people that have been left to be looked over and bought by strangers. In a time when photography was far more difficult and expensive than it is now, someone had once thought the subject important enough to want to preserve their image. These were people who were loved, yet had since been forgotten, and no one was keeping their memories safe. I later discovered from an archivist friend that these found photos are actually known as orphan images. I thought perhaps I would use them as inspiration for projects or stories, that even if I didn't know who they were I could rehome their photos, adopt them, and they could live again, just a little.

I slowly began to amass a gallery of cats and their owners, from Edwardian England to recent times. Sometimes there was a name scrawled in spidery ink on the back of the photos of the pets I found, but of course these animals would not exist in official records like their human family would. I know how much pets are part of a family, how important they are to their owner's life, but more often than not, their companionship, their contribution to family life, is lost to history.

Who were these cats? What were their personalities like? We, as humans, have graves and epitaphs and obituaries, but with the exception of neglected garden markers and posh Victorian pet cemeteries, pets are not memorialised. All these lost characters – all that forgotten love, the head nudges and kneading, the calming strokes and playfulness . . . I wanted to do something that would celebrate them in a way they never could be through a grave, so long after death.

I began to think a lot about how these bonds are not widely understood, and how my love for Dylan potentially labelled me – *ah, the Crazy Cat Lady* . . . The women and cats in these photos might have had a bond as deep as mine and Dylan's, and yet for some, these beautiful images of friendship are simply a chance to label these women as lonely and odd. They must be mad and secretly want 15 cats, no one can have married them, they must be lacking – they could even be a witch! It's a peculiar way of interpreting female portraiture – would they have made the same assumptions if the women in these photos were alone or with children?

There was something unsettling in this idea for me. Why is the 'Cat Lady' seen in such negative terms? Is there a reason? Could I find any clues in history? Through research and a creative project, could I do something to redress this negativity, while creating something hopeful for the future? I wanted to explore and reimagine the idea of the Cat Lady through a creative act of remembering, and to build an alternative memorial for these animals and their women.

Nearly five years after Dylan and I found each other, I moved back to Somerset and his old owners let me take him. He was nearly 17 now and they kindly saw that, considering his age and the bond between us, it would be better for him to come with me.

We had another year and a half together before one day, rushing back from work with a feeling something was wrong, I went up to my room to find him lying at the top of the stairs. He had been coming down to greet me, making one last attempt to see me, when his body had given up and he had died. He was still warm. The urine his dying body had released still bubbled on the surface of the carpet. He had been fine when I'd left that morning. On our last night together he had danced to Kate Bush with me – his old man party trick whenever 'Wuthering Heights' was played. He was certainly old for a cat, but only a little stiff. If only I had known . . .

I know they say cats like to go off quietly and die alone, but I couldn't forgive myself for not being there, for not cuddling up to him on his last day. For not being with him until the end. I think I missed his last breaths by seconds. In that moment my world fell apart.

II I never thought I'd become a Cat Lady. But, as I think of it now, the strangest thing is that it is something you can *become*. You don't *become* a dog or a rabbit lady, it is not seen as odd to keep horses or hamsters. In fact, few creatures have the power to define you as cats do. If I had chosen a different pet – for example, my childhood tortoise, which I still have – perceptions of me would not change. I would be the same. But Cat Lady is a thing. It is an identity.

When we call someone a Cat Lady we imply that they have left acceptable society, become unhinged, mentally unwell and desexualised; Cat Ladies have crossed over to an existence in which normal human relationships become inconceivable. It is something to be feared, as once it has happened it is unlikely to be reversed. It is a transformation. It is an end.

I've purposely chosen the term 'Cat Women' to refer to people in this book. (Though interestingly, Catwoman is both the most sexualised and untrustworthy of female comic book characters.) The word 'lady' implies someone genteel, yet when it follows the word 'cat', it often means the opposite.

For the women who have cats, their relationship with their animal is a positive and beneficial thing. So where does this suspicion that cats can signify or bring about some sort of strange transformation in a woman's being come from? Why, as I reached my fortieth year, did my ownership of cats label me more than what I did for a living, what I had achieved or, on an even more superficial note, what I looked like? Outward appearance of success or sense of sanity can be undermined by being single with cats. Why is it OK, seen as benign, to laugh at Cat Ladies when it's clearly endorsing a sexist stereotype? We don't say, 'He's a man with a dog – beware!' We say, 'Ah, man's best friend! Who wouldn't want to meet a nice man who owns dogs?' Dogs are friends, acceptable companions. Cats, however, are something else entirely . . .

Prejudices like this don't come from nowhere – to become so deep-seated they develop over time. Something in the idea was old

– I could feel it. I spread out my pictures of unknown women with their cats and decided I needed to know more.

In ancient cultures, cats and women had a special relationship – not one to be feared and suspicious of, but one to celebrate and be in awe of. Famous women associated with cats were not lonely old women or witches, but rather goddesses.

In ancient Egypt, cats were revered and there were numerous female cat deities, most notably Bast, whose cult survived for 2,000 years until it was banned in AD 390. Bast was the goddess of maternity and fertility, a part of womanhood to be celebrated, not feared. Cats were also cherished pets, as we can see both in the surviving art of the period and by the thousands of cat mummies that have been found in archaeological expeditions.

In Norse mythology, the goddess of fertility, motherhood and love was Freyja, a powerful goddess again associated with cats, her favoured form of transport being a chariot pulled by two, possibly Norwegian Forest, cats.

There are other examples in various pagan cultures of an association of cats with a mother goddess and the moon with its cycles, and therefore an endless sense of new life. Their nine lives do not necessarily just mean they are good at getting out of tricky situations. The game cat's cradle even has its origins in this idea – you weave a net with your fingers to catch the sun in the form of a little cat, so that it returns with greater strength in the spring. It is a spell in the form of a children's game – a home for miniature magic cats.

To see a black cat or a rainbow brings luck, but if a cat crosses in front of a wedding procession, beware.

A cat is often thrown into a new house to appease the vengeful spirits that haunt any new building.

If illness strikes a house, soak the household cat with water that has been used to wash a patient and then drive it out of doors – the cat will take the illness with him.

Cats can smell the coming wind and raise one if they like, so, like witches, they often do so, especially if offended.

Dogs, cats and horses can all see ghosts, but while most animals are afraid of them, cats are not.

There are many mentions of cats in UK folklore – black cats are sometimes good luck; all cats can notoriously call up a storm, hence why sailors should never throw them overboard. In fact, that is what cats are doing when they scratch at carpets and furniture – not marking territory and destroying your house but controlling the weather. If a cat sits with their back to a fire it is sure to rain. An exploration of the partly fifteenth-century Hay Hall in Birmingham found a cat and mouse to have been built into the walls – possibly to ward off mice in the new building. Cats were different, uncanny; they were intrinsically objects of suspicion in a way that other animals were not.

Yet in early medieval times cats, as far as we can tell, led relatively straightforward lives. There are recorded instances of them being kept as pets by religious orders, including by nuns – our first known Cat Women – and they were valued throughout society for their ability to catch vermin. But this changed in the later medieval period, and what followed are hundreds of years of suspicion and persecution, which often caused trouble for any woman who cared for them.

The role of cats in folklore and ancient religion may have been to their detriment in the early Christian world. Primitive beliefs had to be refuted, so a creature so anciently associated with pre-Christian customs was likely to be persecuted. It was also, specifically, a creature linked to women and female deities within these ancient beliefs, which perhaps strengthened the suspicion of women in relation to cats.

Attitudes really begin to change for the worse in the thirteenth century, when certain links between cats and heresy became stronger. There was a resurgence in the worship of the Norse goddess Freyja by a pagan fertility cult in the Rhineland that caused much consternation. Heretical demonic sects were said to worship cats as a form of the devil. Whatever the reasons, from this time onwards there appears to have been widespread persecution of cats.

There are some incredibly distressing incidences of cats being persecuted. One of the most grizzly is a report that, during the coronation of Elizabeth I in 1559, extreme Protestants filled a wicker effigy of the pope with live cats and burnt it on a pyre – the cats' screams were said to be the language of the devil as it resided in he body of the pope, escaping into the air. Some, in the era of Charles II, were also rather fond of this practice, purportedly using the howls of burning cats to intensify the dramatic effect of anti-heresy protests and other such events.

So the suspicion of cats was embedded into the Western psyche, starting with early Christianity's desire to wipe out pagan beliefs and developing into cats as a symbol for heresy. This all seems a long way from our progressive, science-based, modern beliefs though. Or does it? Is the derisory image of the Cat Lady where the last of this fear and mistrust still left in our unconscious has come to reside?

Where the suspicion of women who have cats becomes dangerous is in the case of witches. Just as the thirteenth century saw the rise in cat persecution, so it also saw a rise in the persecution of cat-owning women that lasted well into the eighteenth century. There are two parts to the belief in this darker relationship – metamorphosis and familiars.

Witches can turn into cats. Sometimes hares and other creatures, but cats, it was believed, are a common choice of creature to metamorphose into. Stories supporting this myth abound. In 1718, it was recorded that a William Montgomery killed two cats and wounded many others who were howling all night. He attacked them fiercely with a sword and a hatchet and two women died the next day. A further woman was found to have a mysterious deep hatchet wound, the damaged limb later withering and dropping off. Many cruelties carried out on cats were the next day justified by suspicious women found supposedly injured in corresponding ways; this confirmed that she was a witch who had transformed into a cat and therefore she (and the cat) had got what she deserved.

Gervase of Tilbury noted in his *Oria Imperialia* of c. 1211 that 'women have been seen and wounded in the shape of cats by persons who were secretly on the watch and . . . the next day the women have shown wounds and loss of limbs.' This was not a short-lived fad, a weird, temporary superstition or quickly refuted ignorance, but a centuries-long belief. When something is believed for this long it embeds itself in society – women would have been wary of being associated with cats for fear of being accused.

During their trials, women accused of metamorphosis were often said to have achieved it through vile ointments that included ingredients such as boiled babies. These horrible and graphic claims added layers of poison onto the innocent lives of women and cats.

But, still, this is not so much a woman *with* cat who is being targeted, as woman *as* cat. It is with the idea of familiars that the danger of women with cats really becomes apparent.

In folklore, a familiar is a demonic creature – not the devil himself, but a gift given by the devil on initiation into witchcraft. They come in the form of small beasts, often a domestic animal, which of course often means a cat. They are not the embodiment of a witch (unlike metamorphosis), but rather a powerful being in their own right, there to help a witch carry out her nefarious magic. Like a much more sinister version of Gobbolino, the witch's cat, in the children's book of the same name, with her sparking whiskers – familiars are the origin of the witch's cat on a broomstick (though why in modern witch stereotypes these are often black I do not know, as black cats in folklore were the only ones with some positive aspect – i.e. being lucky). But to the medieval mind, and for many people well into the eighteenth century, these were not fictional characters but a real and sinister demonic power. A threat. For a woman, being seen with a cat could be a dangerous business.

Keeping animals as household pets was not common practice in the Middle Ages, except in monastic orders or as mousers. In medieval bestiaries (compendiums of real and what we would now see as mythical creatures), cats are nearly always depicted with a mouse or rat. In Europe, cats were not generally kept as pets until the seventeenth century and not till the nineteenth century were cats sentimentalised as cherished pets, mainly among the upper classes. (This is shown by art, the first pet shows and pet cemeteries. Interestingly this growing sentimentality and permission to care openly for pets was likely to have been caused by the increase in rational thinking in the late eighteenth century – the superstitions that led to persecution of cats were now culturally frowned upon.) Therefore stroking or talking to a cat was seen as odd behaviour, and could arouse suspicion. Pre-nineteenth century, aside from the aristocracy, women's lives were largely confined to the home unless helping in the fields, and among these women it was the elderly, the single, the lonely and the widowed who were the most likely to befriend a cat, and therefore most likely to be persecuted. Today it is still women who fall into these categories who are most likely to be stigmatised as a Cat Lady.

At the height of the witch persecutions in the seventeenth century, Cat Women found themselves in grave danger. An account from the Bideford witch trials in 1682 where a witness reports that he saw a cat jump through a woman's window at twilight was enough to get her accused of witchcraft: it was believed that the cat was her familiar.

There are even cases of celebrity familiars, for example a white spotted cat called Sathan, who was widely reported on and talked about in the sixteenth century. Belonging to Elizabeth Francis, who was put on trial for witchcraft in Chelmsford in 1556, Sathan was also a suspiciously old cat, inherited from the accused witch's grandmother – it was thought that familiars were passed from mother to daughter, the one thing it would seem that could be inherited down the female side of the family. Fed on bread, milk and the occasional drop of Elizabeth's blood, Sathan reportedly spoke in a strange hollow voice and did her evil bidding – killing a man who refused to marry her, before procuring her another. After sixteen years she passed him on to Agnes Waterhouse, who used him to kill other people's cattle and a man who had offended her. Agnes herself was then tried for witchcraft in Chelmsford, the same cat therefore being used to condemn at least two innocent women.

This prejudice was not just a European thing. In America the puritanical heritage of the fear of cats was imported with Western settlers. While some Native American cultures saw the native cats as powerful beings (indeed in what is now Illinois an ancient bobcat was found in a burial mound normally reserved for humans, wearing a special collar), small domestic cats are not native to the USA and were imported with settlers when the controlling of vermin became an issue. As in the UK they were kept as mousers, but there are also records of religious extremists persecuting cats for being connected to the devil.

During the Salem witch trials of 1692–3, cats were again suspected of being familiars. This was a moment of intense hysteria, and other animals, including two dogs actually accused of witchcraft themselves, were persecuted. However, other dogs were used to track witches down, suggesting that in general dogs were trusted where cats were not.

Black cats were more feared, and this can be seen continuing through the American creative psyche, with Edgar Allan Poe, fond of cats himself, using the black cat in his dark stories in the first half of the nineteenth century, understanding the negative connotations it would stir up.

Reading accounts of familiars, there is a real sense of perceived threat in the combination of woman and cat. These days we might not believe in witchcraft, but there is still a sense that this threat simmers in a society that does not like women who don't fit into its idea of what women should be. And women who prefer the company of cats do not fit. Today these Cat Ladies are often given the prefix 'Crazy', adding the stigma of mental health issues too.

When I think about these poor women accused of witchcraft just for having a pet, I cannot help but wonder as to what these cats were like. Were they lap cats or aloof? Good hunters? Did they like to play or curl up by the fire? How many feline friendships were destroyed over this sinister ignorance? Thinking back further than my photos can stretch, I like to imagine them: tabby, tortoiseshell, ginger, black or white; jumping, stretching, scratching. I bet they were well loved. And yet, in searching for a saucer of milk or a warm place to sleep, some got their kind female friends killed.

Do not underestimate the fear people had of witches. I am starting to think it is why 'Crazy Cat Lady' is the oldest, and historically most sinister, anti-female label of all . . . how many other modern derogatory terms once led to death sentences?

Of all domestic animals, cats seem to have the most developed sense of their own world, their own lives; they go off and do their thing and we do not know what that is – even the cosiest lap cat is never truly a domesticated animal. There is always that hint of the wild, the unruly. They are independent. You cannot train them like a dog, or herd them like farm animals.

Historically, unruly women were frowned upon, and to this day women that do not fit with society's idea of what they should be suffer distrust or abuse. I remember as a teenager discovering the fictional Wife of Bath, one of literature's great unruly women. We were studying Chaucer's *Canterbury Tales* for GCSE and the idea that this was the fictional voice of a medieval woman from my home city, before the Georgian times that made Bath what it is today, when there were little streets that bore no resemblance to the golden stone grand crescents I knew, was fascinating.

The unfamiliar tang of Old English, tasted for the first time, rolled clumsily around my mouth as I tried out its cadences. I was struck by how she was an untameable woman, and the image of her red stockings, like bloody sunset legs, shocking and bright, stuck in my mind. But it wasn't until I reread it years later that I noticed her unruliness was compared to that of a cat.

'And once you said I was like a cat,' she says to her husband in Nevill Coghill's translation, before referring to how cats were singed to stop them leaving the house, and that men think a woman ought to be kept similarly under control or she would go out 'a-caterwauling' – essentially looking for a mate.

In place of the pagan tradition of celebrating feline deities as symbols of fertility and love, now the cat is a symbol of promiscuity and lust – a byword for a dangerous type of woman who was out of control.

As I have mentioned, nuns and aristocratic women were the two groups free to keep a cat without negative or dangerous connotations. Nuns were immune to being accused of witchcraft and heresy, so this makes sense, yet I still find it interesting. While revered, nuns did not fit with societal expectations of women. Educated, without children or a husband, they were as such 'un-female'; it was their marriage to Christ that protected them from heretical suspicion. So it seems the only woman who could be a Cat Lady completely safely was one seen as spiritually pure. Virginal.

Aristocratic Cat Women were protected by their status. There are some interesting examples, such as Frances Stuart, Duchess of Richmond, who on her death in 1702 bequeathed a legacy for the upkeep of her cats. Also, Catherine the Great, whose cats' descendants still inhabit the Hermitage Museum in St Petersburg today, where a woman known as the 'cat mother' looks after them. In the eighteenth century, feted French harp player Mademoiselle Dupuy tried to leave her two houses to her cats (though this was overturned in court on her death). However, these women were notable exceptions. In general, until the nineteenth century, and certainly in the UK, the preference was for dogs and horses. Cats were never quite as socially acceptable in aristocratic circles, and even when this started to change in the nineteenth century, it was pure breeds that drew the interest of the well-to-do, not moggies. At the first cat show at the Crystal Palace in 1871, a working-class woman with a beautiful ordinary cat would have not been allowed to enter as the organisers tried to change perceptions of cats as pest exterminators by courting the upper classes. Later cat shows allowed working-class people to enter, but there were separate categories for different social classes as well as breeds.

III   Cat Women aren't a peculiarly English thing, though the term Cat Lady is particular to the English language. When I ask friends from different countries, though they often recognise the Western concept of a Cat Lady, there is not usually a corresponding term they can give me in their own language. Is this because of our puritanical heritage and the historical persecution of women and cats?

I remember the first time I went to Rome. I had pictured what it would be like – the classical ruins and beautiful people, the buzz and – owing to my taste in films – a certain 1960s glamour. I was 23 and had just come back from travelling in Canada, California and Japan. I was having post-adventure come down, so decided to go and stay with a friend who had recently moved there.

I wandered the streets in the January sunshine, while mopeds sped past me in the pale clear light – motorised bees. I drank strong espresso and sat scribbling among the ruins, and it was during the latter that I noticed the cats.

There were cats everywhere! Great big clowders of cats. They wandered through the ruins, stretching out on stones and grass. This was their terrain. I had never seen anything like it in England, where the stray is a sad lonely character.

And then I noticed something else. Gazing down at the Coliseum I saw an old lady hobble up before scattering cat food everywhere. In many countries, a feral cat population that took over a historic monument would be seen as something to exterminate, or hopefully rescue, but here they were left to their domain and fed. I went back repeatedly and every time the feeder was an old lady – the ideal candidate for the Crazy Cat Lady of English preconceptions, yet this felt different.

There is a lovely eccentric 1953 film, *Confidenze di un Gatto*, of the cats of Rome, narrated in Italian by a cat, and in one section the ladies (and one man and one dog with a steak hanging out of his mouth like a fleshy butterfly) are feeding the cats in the ruins of the Fori Imperiali near the Coliseum. It is a positive film – one of sunshine and playfulness without negative connotations.

I rewatched it recently online and stared intently at the women feeding the cats, trying to read their faces. They stand there distributing their food and the cats gather to make a swirling train – I can almost picture a vintage fashion plate with an illustration of an Italian woman casually leaning on a ruin, a moving dress of live wild cats, a living outfit.

A couple of the women are not that old, unlike all the women I saw there in the early 2000s. I wondered if the youngest could be the lady I saw 50 years later, or perhaps she was the daughter of one of these Roman Cat Women in the film. Perhaps these cats of Rome are passed down matrilineally, just like the Puritans feared of a witch's familiar. This image – the paper (now plastic) bags of food scattered round for these clamouring clowders – seems timeless. Cats don't date like clothes do, or the colour of film.

Tbilisi, Georgia, is my favourite city, and one where I have spent many months. Here too I was fascinated by the street cats.

I remember wandering up a darkened street at night and seeing a group of them waiting in a courtyard. The cats slowly gathered, knowing exactly where to be and when. Finally, an old lady with a carrier bag appeared and fed them. It felt like I'd gatecrashed a magic midnight feast.

On another occasion, down in the old town – daytime now – cats of every colour gathered as another older lady appeared and made neat little piles of dried food so each cat could reach some. It was obviously a regular occurrence.

It was strange. Always old ladies – yes, the expected cliché – but they didn't have the air of the lonely Crazy Cat Lady in her messy home covered in cats. My presumption was these ladies had immaculate homes and many grandchildren. More interestingly, the relationship seemed to be one of caretaker of the cats. These women were not consumed by the catness, replacing what was missing in their lives, but somehow doing something that was expected and good – there was a reverence or duty to it. They didn't take them home, didn't even stop and stroke them particularly, or sit down on a bench and try to make them jump up onto their laps. No neediness, no projecting on to them. They simply fed and admired them, and then went about the rest of their day. I couldn't help but think how such brazen, open-air caring for cats could have got them into trouble in centuries past – they would have been labelled witches in England for sure. Here they were, old and a little eccentric, but mostly kind. And not defined by their relationship with the cats.

I tried to picture this back home. If the centre of a historic city like Bath or York got overtaken by cats and they were fed by old ladies, would this behaviour be looked on as kind, or unremarkable, or would we instantly label them as Crazy Cat Ladies?

You become a Cat Lady when you hit middle age, yet some of the strongest bonds, as seen again and again in my found photos, are between young girls and cats, young women too. It is an ageless bond, but it doesn't attract a label until there is something else society deems suspicious in your life, especially if you are past childbearing age and/or have no husband . . . Does it say something about how in Western and Northern European societies we view female ageing? Are older women more venerated in other cultures, where Cat Lady as identity is not such a thing?

Historically the cat has been revered more in some cultures than others, particularly the Middle and Near East. While Western Christian societies were suspicious of cats, Muslim cultures cared for them. It is even reported that the Prophet Muhammad cut off his sleeve so as not to disturb a sleeping cat.

Today predominantly Muslim countries are more cat than dog cultures. In Turkey, Istanbul has a park where stray cats are protected and the street cats feel like an integral part of the spirit of the city, and there is a cat village in Antalya with hammocks and tree houses for 100 strays.

In Hindu culture, cats were also cherished. There is again, as in Egyptian and Norse culture, a goddess with feline connections – Shashthi, goddess of maternity and children, who rides a cat and, in ancient depictions, sometimes has a cat face. Indeed the adopting and looking after of a cat is theoretically part of being an orthodox Hindu.

In Buddhism, the cat is also historically venerated. If a Buddhist is at a sufficiently spiritually advanced point when they die their soul may go into a cat, and when that cat dies their soul will enter paradise. There is also a tradition of temple cats, and in what is now Myanmar and Thailand the Burmese and Siamese cats were highly prized. Japan too respected cats; the first documented kittens were born in the imperial court in the year 999 and from that point onwards cats were treated like lapdogs and walked on leads, only being released for a wilder life when the rodent population got out of control in the seventeenth century. Indeed, today, feeding stray cats is said to bring wealth and good fortune and there are a number of 'cat islands', such as Tashirojima and Aoshima, where cats significantly outnumber humans, which are tourist attractions. The maneki-neko, more commonly known as the beckoning cat, is an iconic symbol of Japan and said to bring good luck. I wonder if in a culture that was anti-Cat Lady, whether even the pop culture icon that is Hello Kitty would have materialised as a different creature – a dog or a pony perhaps.

IV Without doubt, dogs are intrinsically 'male' and cats 'female'. Dogs are not seen as a problematic pet for women, yet linguistically they are – to call a woman a bitch or a dog is a misogynistic insult. To say *you old dog* to a man can be a way to suggest approval of lascivious behaviour. It comes with a nudge and another beer. Men are never described in feline terms, unless in a camp cliché.

Cat-derived language is often a way of demeaning or sexualising women: women 'purr' when aroused for the benefit of men, wear kitten heels for cuteness or are described as kittenish when playing the coquette. Yet at the same time, women who own cats are seen to have renounced their sexuality, to have chosen feline companionship over the potential for a sexual relationship with a (let's face it, male) mate.

Yet language that references cats is not just used to sexualise women, it can also suggest suspicion of women's nature. Only women are 'catty'. This word denotes a peculiarly 'feminine' form of meanness – men might say horrible things but be seen as more straightforward, more direct. Historically women were seen as gossips and gossiping was a sin. Cattiness and gossiping go hand in hand. To be catty is to be deceitful, to speak behind someone's back. When a woman says something critical – usually specifically of another woman – it's not unheard of for someone to say 'meow'. When it comes to writing, however, there are many famous cat men who do not suffer for their feline fondness. The infamously macho Ernest Hemingway adored cats and at his house had enough to make any woman fall squarely into the category of Crazy Cat Lady. Yet Hemingway is not seen as any less manly for his admiration for the animals. Perhaps it helps that the cats were unusual – they were polydactyl, meaning they had six toes, and were reportedly all descended from Snow White – a sailor's cat given to him. Sailors tended to favour this genetic mutation as it purportedly helped with mousing and stability on ship. Let's for a moment imagine a woman with a clowder of six-toed cats becoming an increasingly introverted writer – witch alert! But Hemingway remains the role model for a certain literary macho type, and the descendants of his six-toed cats still inhabit his house – now a museum – today. Maybe boozing and bullfighting is simply sufficient to cancel out Crazy Cat Man.

Raymond Chandler had a particularly good cat helper, Take, who practised the fine art of sitting on manuscripts in progress. William S. Burroughs wrote an autobiographical book, *The Cat Inside,* exploring his own life through his many cats. He even casts them as a version of familiars – though he sees them as spirit guides in dreams, rather than the demonic companion of the true term.

As with Hemingway, these writers' Cat Man-ness does not affect their reputation. In fact, it is seen as interesting because they are otherwise counterculture or manly writers. It probably wouldn't be worth mentioning had they liked dogs, but the feminine weakness or eccentricity of cat love apparently adds to the intrigue in a way it really wouldn't if they had been women.

Seventeen years after publishing his seminal work of modernist poetry *The Wasteland*, T.S. Eliot wrote *Practical Cats*, first under the pseudonym of Old Possum, a series of light-hearted poems personifying cats, purportedly to entertain his godchildren. Charles Bukowski – once dubbed 'the laureate of the lowlife' – was passionate about his cats, and there is a posthumously published poetry collection of his writing on cats. In fact, most of the well-known (or, at least, critically regarded) creative works on cats are by men. Indeed it was the publication of *Les Chats* by Francois Auguste Paradis de Moncrief in 1727 that started to change attitudes, especially amongst fashionable men, on the continent. Yet it is women that are labelled by their catness.

Do artistic women similarly get away with being cat lovers without suspicion? From Colette to Angela Carter to Joyce Carol Oates, many female writers have an affinity for cats, and while today that certainly wouldn't see anyone persecuted, it seems unlikely to help elevate them to cult figure status. I'd like to think that people just don't see it as relevant to their writing, but I also wonder whether if, as a woman, and a creative one at that (it is perhaps unruly by definition to be a creative woman), it is ever truly safe to come out as a Cat Woman, to let that description in? No matter how proud we might be of it, no matter how benign the resultant teasing might be, the more sinister connotations – the witchcraft and the prophesy of solitude and squalor; the hint of potential madness – simmer away.

V Struggling with my grief when Dylan died, I noticed that while many adults mistrusted it, children understood straight away. They didn't think it odd that it had affected me so deeply. They also loved the photos I had collected when I showed them.

People often underestimate the bond between children and their pets. Working on creative projects in schools for many years, I have lost count of the number of times I have been told about a favourite dog, cat or hamster, or been shown a shrine to a sadly departed guinea pig. These bonds are how we learn to love beyond our parents and siblings, our first taste of the responsibility of another's life, the way we first experience and make sense of grief. As children, pets are also often our dear friends – when young, we don't feel that we shouldn't talk to animals for fear of seeming strange. In many of the photos in this book, cats are often playmates for children – someone who understands your adventures and inner imaginary world; a companion in the wildest adventures of make-believe.

One of my favourite famous examples of the bond between girl and cat is a fictional one from children's television, but no less real somehow. The friendship between Emily and Bagpuss is one of the most touching portraits of what the dynamic between cat and girl can be. She the loving friend, he the wise and kind older creature, looking out for his dear owner. He does his best to help – she brings him lost objects, then overnight he works with the other toys to bring them to life again. A metaphor for the healing power of pets perhaps. He never takes credit – she doesn't know that it is he who organises the fixing of things. In fact, she doesn't see him come to life at all, but still she loves him.

I never cease to be moved by the description of Bagpuss: he was a 'saggy old cloth cat loose at the seams', always followed by the line that melts me – 'but Emily loved him'. It reminds me of Dylan as he got older and frail, skinnier with looser skin, but the bond was stronger than ever. And there was a childlike fierceness to it – me and him against the world . . .

As we grow into adolescence, with all its confusions, pets help us make sense of the world; they hold our hope. I met Dylan as an adult, but the feeling of my time with him, the time of my life that rushes back when I think of the atmosphere of being with him, is oddly reminiscent of my late teens when I first danced in clubs, fell in love with bands, rifled charity shops for glam granny dresses and began to travel the world. The feeling that crashes through me is of how the world back then was so vast, yet seemingly there for the taking – how anything could happen, how all would be OK. This might sound strange, but I think the reason for this is the sense of security and hope he brought me. I felt better when he was around, and the bond reminded me of the feeling we have in youth before the worries of adult life have taken over. I felt not so much dependent on him, but stronger because of him – optimistic.

Society often sees pets, especially cats owned by older women or even shy children, as being an emotional crutch, filling a gap in a life left vacant by human contact. But to me this is a false way of seeing. The joy of a relationship with an animal is as much about the future of a life together, or a secret companion in what could be. They are a representation of hope, not resigned failure.

In today's world of social media it is hard as a teenage girl to avoid photos of yourself or unrealistic images of others. Things have changed hugely since the 1980s and 90s of my youth and I am so thankful I grew up before this pressure. In terms of the history of female portraiture, true awkward adolescence is one of the more under-represented areas – portraits were generally, although of course not exclusively, painted of children or grown women. There is the posed debutante, but painted or photographic portraits of teenage girls in natural moments are scarce – they sit in the realm of artistic licence rather than formal portraiture.

In my day, adolescence was the time to avoid cameras like the plague, and I am not the only one who felt this – in my collection of photos, those of teenagers or adolescent girls are the scarcest, yet those I have found have proved some of the most moving. Would the photo have been taken at all if it were not for them being lost in the moment with their cat, or wanting to have their beloved feline friend recorded for posterity? They might have felt that they would live forever, but their pet ... at all ages there is a poignancy in the fleetingness of pet lives. The girls' future may have been wide open, but their cats would not be there to see it through.

Though we might feel physically awkward at times, our teenage years can be both when we explore the outside world most thoroughly, and through our intense friendships and imaginings create the most vivid interior world we may ever have. This is the age when we write diaries, devising secret codes for people we come across socially. This is when we can have a relationship with our pet free of the accusation of Cat Lady – perhaps not even knowing what the expression means. Yet here the bond is no less intense; the cat can feature as an ally in this vivid interior world as much as a good friend can.

Cats are sensitive creatures, they pick up on moods, and so I wonder if they enter this dreaminess too? Is there something different in the expressions of the cats in these photos with their teenage owners – are they part of this excitement, this wistful optimism, or conversely the depths of despair when things don't turn out as planned? Is it a place of thought magic cats are quite comfortable in?

The love women feel for cats is irrefutable. But do cats love us back? In a recent documentary, scientists observed cats and dogs sat with their owners in a room. When the owners left the dogs pined, while the cats didn't seem that bothered. When the owner came back into the room the dogs were joyous; the cats remained unconcerned.

Cats are notoriously independent; that they are rarely needy is one of the things people love about them – if they are affectionate it is because they choose to be. Yet to confuse this independence with indifference I think is to misunderstand cat behaviour.

Love is by its nature an indefinable thing. How do we know when we fall in love? We just do. There is no proof or measurement – it is a thing of instinct, of gut feeling. If animals are ruled by instinct, and love is something intangible and immeasurable – beyond looking at hormone reactions in the body, chemicals in the brain – then I do not see why animals couldn't have their own version of love. I am not a scientist, but I wonder if it is not that they don't love, so much that they love differently. Who are we as humans to know how another species feels?

All cat owners know about cupboard love – that moment when a cat acts besotted as they know it might get them food. But while motivated affection, this nevertheless shows an intelligent understanding of what constitutes kind and loving behaviour to humans.

How would we define love? If it is a feeling of comfort, then cats when worried or ill will often be more affectionate or curl up close. Cuddling – well we do not cuddle those we don't care for and cats definitely cuddle. And there is the individuality of love – we do not love all people in our lives, so why should all cats love all people, or even, I hate to say, all owners. I love the two cats I have now and, in their very individual ways, I know they are very fond of me. The adventurous one, Tariel, can appear indifferent, but will come straight to me and no one else if worried or poorly. My little farm stray Sindri is somewhat clingy, hiding from everyone but snuggling up to me. Yet if I am honest I know they do not love me as much as Dylan did.

Yet for all these 'symptoms' of love that cat owners claim, there are always the horror stories. Have you heard the one about the little old lady who died alone and no one discovered her for weeks, by which point her cats had started to eat her? I would say that such urban myths are a symptom of our fear of Cat Ladies. Or our inherent human dread of ending up alone, and unloved.

Or what about the celebrity cases that prove the point? Today some of the most famous cases of Cat Ladies come from America, such as Edith Bouvier Beale, society model and aunt of Jackie Kennedy, who refused to leave her Long Island home, Grey Gardens (subject of the 1976 film of the same name), living with her daughter in increasingly squalid conditions with many cats. If she had been living with a menagerie of other animals, would the disgust in the change in her life have been so extreme? The shock might still have been there, but do the cats add something extra to the horror of the situation?

People are keen to point out the flaws of cats, but it is dogs that more often (although still rarely) attack and kill humans. I would argue that there is something else at work here, something that goes back to historical suspicions.

Indeed a recent study by the University of California, Los Angeles, found no evidence that cat owners differ from others, including dog owners, in terms of depression, anxiety or relationship experiences. As far as I can tell the study wasn't gendered, but rather of 561 people. Yet still the newspaper I read about it in had Crazy Cat Lady in the headline, and those who carried out the study when commenting referred to the Cat Lady stereotype. The fact that a prestigious university felt the need to undertake such a study, that it was scientifically warranted, in itself says something about how deeply ingrained the stereotype is.

Cat Lady – a spectre of loneliness and squalor, who lives by herself in poverty with tens of cats – remains the epitome of sad and lonely female failure. That is how you end up eaten by your pets – not because cats are inherently callous and that's what they'd do, but because that's what you should expect if you lead a life without a husband and children. This is obviously not true, but the cliché remains. In my experience, true love of an animal can lead to enormous grief, but no failing – just the tragedy of the loss of love like any other.

For every relationship of indifference, for every unrequited devotion, there is also reciprocal love, the love that may have lain at the heart of my photos. And if it was there, it deserves a chance to be seen again, to be celebrated and valued as the legitimate love that it was. From Classical literature to Shakespeare to the Brontës, great love stories are creatively reimagined all the time. Doesn't a person's love for a pet deserve recognition too? Just because it can be hard for some to understand in human terms, just because it was not romantic love, does not mean that it was not true.

VI The photos in this book are portraits. Some are formal – you can notice that the clothes have been carefully picked out, the gaze is firmly trained on the camera, the cat or new kitten is held out for proud display. Others are more natural, more candid – a moment caught without the self-consciousness of formal portraiture, but a portrait none the less.

In the very early days of photography, the new equipment required a posing that was shorter than but still as formal as sitting for a painter. You had to sit completely motionless, in case this magical new equipment lost focus and blurred.

Portraits, both in terms of painting and later photography, are the images of us left when we depart the world, and which people we have not met will know us by. They are also the images we look back on in later life to say 'that is what I was like'. So this forced, posed, moment becomes not just a picture but a definition of our identity – a record – an archive for the fleetingness of time. This is image as curation of self.

But with our animals, while we may know how we want to remember them, we cannot control them in the same way. People try today – dressing up their pets hoping for social media cult status – but in terms of portraiture we can only really capture how the animal chooses to be in that moment, and they are not thinking of posterity.

A person makes a choice to be portrayed with an animal, but that is arguably where they lose control of exactly how the image will come out. There is an inherent unexpected quality, and this interaction between self-controlling human and uncontrollable animal gives a clue to personality it can be hard to see in a formal human-only image. We can see more in the faces of the women in this book as they hold their beloved cats than we perhaps would have done if the cats weren't there.

Cats appear early in art, not just in ancient Egyptian and Far Eastern culture, but in the UK in bestiaries and other ancient manuscripts, as shown in Kathleen Walker-Meikle's wonderful *Cats in Medieval Art*, published by the British Library. Yet portraits of women and cats are scarce in medieval times – I could find but one that seemed like portraiture, and a domestic rather than a stylised or iconographic scene. A Netherlandish Hours of the Virgin manuscript illustrated in the thirteenth or fourteenth century contains an image of a nun with a cat playing with a spindle as she winds it up. It is a markedly different type of image to other portrayals in medieval manuscripts, which show cats almost exclusively as mousers, in that it suggests a relationship between them – an ordinary playful friendship between a woman and a cat.

As we move into later centuries, it was not unusual to have your portrait painted with an animal, though in the UK these were usually beloved hounds – an animal hugely treasured and without the historical negative connotations of their feline counterparts. Outside of the UK, there are some amazing examples of women and cat portraits.

One of the most beautiful to my mind is Francesco Bacchiacca's Portrait of a Young Lady Holding a Cat from the sixteenth century. The young woman stares sideways out at us; rather than coy though, her glance is slightly cheeky, her mouth almost curling to a smile. Yet as I stare longer I sense a wariness. I let my eyes trail down to her hands that hold her tabby cat tightly and there seems a challenge there. The cat is gazing off into the distance, unsurprisingly refusing to stare at the painter, but her grip and steady sidewards gaze give me a glimpse into their relationship – yes, there is the danger he could run away if not held tightly, but he is not at her side, being played with, demurely sitting on her lap. He is held to her. He is held close in a way only that which we hold most dear would be.

Another interesting European work is from a time when in the UK women with cats were at risk of being persecuted. David Rijkaert III's Peasant Woman with a Cat, painted in the 1640s, is a Netherlandish genre scene. It is unusual in that it depicts a non-aristocratic older women, and therefore a prime candidate for suspicious Cat Lady, spoon-feeding a cat wrapped in a blanket. There is an affection here that is moving to see, as well as a little humour. However, this is an allegorical scene from everyday life, not a formal portrait of a real woman, capturing her with her cat for posterity.

As we reach the nineteenth century and society's general perception of pet and especially cat painting has changed, we see many more portraits of women and cats. On the one hand, we begin to see a large number of sentimentalised scenes of young girls playing with kittens, of the type most familiar to us now from biscuit tins and old-fashioned greetings cards. Yet we also see wonderful portraits emerge, such as Renoir's Woman with a Cat of 1895. It is also in this century that Manet illustrated Champfleury's *Les Chats*. Yet as the *fin de siècle* was reached, there was one painter of cats whose work stands out like a beacon for its true understanding of the depth of the bond between women and cats. The painter was herself a British woman misunderstood in terms of her identity as a Cat Lady, but in my opinion she is one of the finest painters of the twentieth century: Gwen John.

If there was a canon of Cat Ladies, Gwen John would seem one of the most tragic cases, dying in 1939 at the age of 63 from self-

neglect, after years of solitude and increasing numbers of pet cats. But to see her in this way I feel is to misunderstand her completely. In jumping to define the tragedy of Gwen John's life in terms of the tropes of the Cat Lady, do we overlook the possibility that her cats were the tonic rather than the tragedy in her life?

Gwen John drew and painted hundreds of cats. In her work, the true personality of ordinary cats simmers on the page, in some of the most tender animal works ever created. She drew cats both alone and with women. Her Young Woman Holding a Cat of 1920 shows a woman in a blue dress deep in thought, her hands clasped around a large black cat on her lap with its back to us. There is no need to try to capture a forced relationship – they are sat together, woman and cat, as comfortable companions, the cat visually and metaphorically a part of her as, held close, it merges into her dress. There is a sadness in the young woman's eyes as she looks into the distance and, while we cannot see the cat's face, we do not need to in order to understand that he is her comfort; while others may not understand, this relationship is one of simply being together.

It is the first time in a portrait of a woman and a cat that I see not a representation of what they looked like so much, or how the artist wanted them to be seen, but the unspoken relationship between them, the tenderness and care, the quiet love. The cat is being good and kind. The young woman is thinking. This is a picture of stillness, of tender tranquillity, yet it is this essence of their relationship that enables me to picture her fingers gently stroking him as they sit. There is no pose, despite her having had to sit still for so long. It is a natural portrait.

Gwen John is usually written about primarily in the context of the men in her life; the cats are cast as an aside to prove her loneliness and eccentricity. Her relationship with her brother, the painter Augustus John, and most of all her love affair with Rodin – an affair which caused her great pain and often hindered her ability to work – seem to define her, and are given more weight than her other choices. In accounts of her life, her Cat Lady behaviour is somehow seen as more unseemly than her obsessive behaviour over Rodin. It appears to be acceptable for a woman to be left distraught by a philandering genius older man, far more so that the decision to surround oneself with lots of cats . . .

This is largely to do with her reclusiveness. Much of what we know of her is from her letters, of which hundreds survive addressed to Rodin. Yet for all her pronouncements of love and her passionate despair at his treatment of her, which we see recorded in these letters, I think we see a deeper level of what I would call love in her reaction to the loss of her beloved cat Tiger. The former might be more interesting to some readers, but I believe the other is more true, more telling.

Gwen loved cats as a child in Wales and this followed her into adulthood in Paris. Gwen and Tiger were incredibly close. She would take her out with her, and some nights they would go out into the Jardin du Luxembourg to sleep in the trees together – it is an extraordinary testament to their bond that Tiger did not run away. In the summer, when Paris got too hot, she would move to the country, again taking Tiger with her, and it is here that I think the most extraordinary testament to love occurs, as related in Susan Chitty's biography.

Gwen had been painting at Rodin's property in Meudon, outside with Tiger, but on the tram on the way home the cat jumped out of the door when spooked, at the village of St Cloud, and disappeared. Gwen was beside herself. She ran through the village, ignoring the ridicule she attracted as she asked everyone if they had seen her cat. Refusing to give up, she wandered through wasteland, past prostitutes and sneering men, without regard for her safety. For nine days she slept outside, searching for Tiger. She laid elaborate trails of meat, hoping she would be tempted and find them, then her. She offered a reward, despite her poverty. She got Rodin to obtain permission for her to search all the private gardens in the area. If refused entry she trespassed at night. She once got her skirt caught climbing a fence and ended up half naked in the street.

Unable to find her, she eventually returned to Paris, but she could not contain her despair. She missed engagements. Then, at her lowest ebb, she received a message that a cat had been spotted. Gwen rushed back and set up camp where she and Tiger had sat painting that first day. She lay there for three days with parcels of meat in her den in the bushes, when Tiger finally returned.

To some this might seem lunacy, but as someone who has truly loved a cat, I understand. I would have done this for Dylan.

They had another few years together before Tiger disappeared again, and tragically this time the cat was not found. Gwen John owned dozens more cats in her life; towards the end she refused to leave the wooden building on a piece of land she owned as she was worried about who would look after the cats.

When I think of Gwen John's life and the story of Tiger, I am not struck by what this says about her loneliness but how it compares to any hundreds of love letters she wrote to Rodin. Her despair and action, the physical risks she took to find her, make love letters and jealousy over a man seem prosaic.

Gwen John did not fit into any box, and in her quiet, solitary way she was unruly. She was complicated and extremely talented, but the fact remains that, for some, 'mad with cats' makes unusual behaviour easier to understand than the complexities of artistic genius, when not in the body of a feted man. We expect Hemingway or Rodin to be eccentric, but women should behave. But when people talk of her extreme loneliness in later life, I do not think the cats contributed to it. In a life of heartbreak, poverty and, yes, loneliness, for me it is her being a Cat Woman that probably provided her most uncomplicated moments of comfort and joy. Her art is a celebration of this – a monument to the true love and characters of cats lost to history. Her legacy should not be love letters to a famous man who treated her badly; she was not a writer but a painter, and it is the latter that is the truest testament to her love and extraordinary talent.

VII   Memory is intangible – vivid yet constantly fading, moving like
wisps of cloud, dissolving on thought-tongues like sugar. How do
we remember? Create a memorial that will allow us to hope that
things we care about will be remembered?

I had a strange experience the other day. After visiting an
animal sanctuary, on the way back to the car I stumbled across a
memorial garden. I had not expected it to be there, but the little
plaques and wooden crosses seemed to call me in. I had been
thinking about including pet cemeteries in this essay, but so far
my research had only turned up information on famous old ones
(Hyde Park in London has a wonderful Victorian one), which
were mainly for dogs. Some contained the odd grave for a cat,
but these still told me nothing of Cat Women or the love and life
of everyday creatures, and seemed only to reflect the increased
sentimental nature of the relationship people had with their pets
in the nineteenth century.

Still, I could not walk past without paying my respects, but as
I curiously walked into the memorial garden, I realised that I had
underestimated my emotional response. Within moments I was
choking, trying to suppress tears.

It was not a cemetery – there were no bodies here, just memories,
some recent, held in words and names scratched on wood and
stone. Sometimes it was hard to tell which plaques were for
people and which for pets – though occasionally they mentioned
a particularly loved horse or dog. I found one cat named Felix and
an image of the woman that owned him floated up through my
imagination. The garden was alive with memory spells, dancing
like dragonflies I could feel but not see. The women and cats in my
photo collection fluttered into my mind.

This was a place of love, a place to save animal memories from
being lost, and put them on an equal footing with the people who
had loved them. I had accidentally found what my research had so
far failed to turn up – a physical place that truly represented the
depth of our friendship with creatures. This memorial seemed to

me to be a vindication of the relationship it is possible to have with animals.

I realised then that the real pet cemeteries weren't the famous ones with actual gravestones, but the lost ones that lie mostly forgotten in gardens all around the world, where the carefully wrapped bodies of pets, ceremonially spoken over by women, men and bereft children, were placed.

When my parents sold the house I grew up in, leaving the graves of decades of pets was one of the hardest things for me – I was terrified the new owners would dig them up. The most poignant thing I found when clearing my childhood room was the pencil scribblings on the 1980s Laura Ashley wallpaper commemorating the date when my goldfish and hamster died.

I got Dylan cremated as I could not bear the knowledge that I might have left him somewhere he would be disturbed. But there must be thousands if not millions of lost pet graves lying under back gardens across the world. Which makes me wonder – did Cat Women in the past secretly bury their beloved friends, afraid of being caught and accused of witchcraft, or simply laughed at for caring so much? How many secret graveyards had I walked over across the years?

I have always been fascinated by the dichotomy between sanctioned universal and personal history, and how the former is so often represented by monuments – abstract structures that provide a physical location for collective grief and remembering, focusing what is remembered arguably to the detriment of the ordinary poignant reality of individual memories. Rather than famous pet cemeteries and therefore the official memorials of the few, where do the memories of the thousands of lost, undocumented friendships I was curious about lie? How can they be remembered?

In the late nineteenth century, despite the growing sentimentalism towards pets, cat mummies that had been dug up in Egyptian excavations were shipped back to the UK and ground up to use as fertilizer. In fields near Liverpool, the ashes of 300,000 ancient Egyptian cats – who must have been revered or cared for, or even loved – were scattered across farms. How many tractors and walkers have trodden the soil anointed with ancient memories? These fields are lost memorials too.

As I walked out of that memorial garden I willed the forgotten stories of the thousands of cats lost under gardens, scattered over land across the world into my brain. In some small way, I wanted the Cat Women (and men) through centuries to know their grief at their lost pets was valued. That I understood.

'I long to have such a memorial of every being dear to me in the world. It is not merely the likeness that is precious in such cases – but the association and the sense of nearness involved in the thing . . . the fact of the *very shadow of the person* lying there fixed forever!'
Elizabeth Barrett, 1843, quoted in Susan Sontag's *On Photography*.

Grief is a frightening word – alone it sounds like a brusque mythical creature. It is an abrupt word, one that on being spoken slices through the air. It does not have a comforting sound, yet his little word is our way of explaining, or labelling, perhaps the most profound emotion any of us will ever experience.

When Dylan died the feelings that followed were something I could never have prepared for. And in those months of confusion, of bewilderment at functioning in a world without him in it, my collection of photos of women and cats took on new meaning. They were photos of joy, tender portrayals of female and cat friendships, yet also perhaps the last embodiment of the memories of these lost creatures. I felt a new responsibility in collecting and studying and then writing about the images – my goal of creating an alternative memorial grew in importance.

Photos are by definition a capturing of one moment in time. We can look at them and imagine a wider story, but they only show a split second in history – they are a long-running visual pause on a moment in the lives of those they show. After the photos were taken, the chances are the women in them would have experienced grief for these cats. Would these images have then gone from a keepsake of everyday life to something much deeper – the only way these women could see their beloved pets once more?

Yet photos are also inadequate – as time distorts memory, they become more abstract. I look at photos of Dylan now and while years on they can instantly bring me to tears, I am also aware of how they are losing their intensity. Looking at the same image over and over again causes the impact to fade, as they do not change – no sudden forgotten movements and quirks pop up to bring him back to me. They have become flat, even though they are still beautiful.

But I still have them. They are my images to cherish. But found photographs, as orphan images, have had a different journey. Starting from that point of belonging they have been set adrift in the world. Perhaps following a house clearance, or because they end up with relatives further down the line who let them pass on, they may pass through junk shops, dealers or even end up in a skip. The images in this book maybe passed through dozens of hands before they found mine . . .

Yet the fact that they still exist also means something. For an unwanted scrap of memory paper to survive is a triumph against the odds – they have not been lost, ended up in landfill, had drinks spilt on them, been torn by careless hands. They have survived air travel in some cases. They have survived the loss of the memories that defined what they were, the passing of those for who they had real meaning. They are both full of memory and yet, in their orphan state, conversely a tabula rasa for who the characters in them might have been.

Reading and viewing are both creative acts. Even though someone else wrote the words or created the image, we still bring our creative thinking into their contemplation – our own stories, ideas, perhaps too our own grief and loss. No two people look at or read something in the same way – no two imaginations are the same. In this way, orphan images are the starting point of a creative act – the moment where the real can become imaginary, where the everyday can take on a new life in the eyes of another.

I felt that there was a great responsibility in such an endeavour. Fragments of lives were scattered across my bed as I scribbled in notebooks, trying to find a hint at who these people and cats could have been. I will never know for sure, of course – I know I will get things wrong. But I hope that, whoever they were, they would understand that my efforts come from a place of celebration, of sadness and understanding, and an urge to use their image's rootlessness to free them for a new life. As my, then the viewers' imaginations create new stories for them, that in turn becomes a new body of memories in mine and the viewers' minds.

Thinking of images and memory led me back to Susan Sontag, whose *On Photography* I loved in my art history student days. There is so much richness, but one of the things she says stands out for me now, with renewed strength: 'Photographs are of course artefacts. But their appeal is that they also seem, in a world littered with photographic relics, to have the status of found objects – unpremeditated slices of the world. Thus, they trade simultaneously on the prestige of art and the magic of the real.'

But when photos actually *are* found objects, not images in art books, how they behave or 'trade' is different. When the photographer is anonymous the power is with the viewer – the anonymity of the photographer allows an easier way in to the everyday magic, without the distance of art. And today, when the world is less and less littered with photographic relics, the word 'relics' seems to take on the greater spiritual meaning that it inherently has. Photos perhaps are no longer just an image of the past, a trigger for nostalgia and memory, but a one-of-a-kind object giving photography as recorded image the rarity of a painting rather than something that is designed for mass production.

Without their 'artist parent' or other factual information, orphan images are freer to speak for themselves, inspire unfiltered imagination and cast the viewer into a creative role – and so the image can access the realm of mass imagination to embody a more universal sense of remembering.

Memory is situated everywhere but nowhere. It moves with us. It disappears to only reappear in unexpected places. I sometimes picture memory as a soft mist, hiding out in secret compartments in our brains, or lurking on street corners waiting to jump out and surprise us.

When I lost Dylan I couldn't remember him as strongly as I wanted to. I felt as if my memory was full of holes, like cartoon cheese, and he rested in them purring, using the gaps like a hammock, stretching out and filling them all up till what had happened was melted and blurry. Yet it was also a vivid time of memory behaving strangely. I remember feeling he was with me in a meeting. And I remember walking in the woods and picking up a bundle of air to place in my rucksack and then continue walking – my invisible dead cat in my rucksack. Memory as physical feeling, not thought.

I felt like I was going mad, but many who experience grief talk of hallucinations or feeling someone is there. Not a ghost as such, but a presence. It is different to an optimistic willing. I could not control when it would feel like he was there.

In *On Photography*, Sontag discusses Proust, who was sceptical of the powers of photography in relationship to memory – for him a photo was too controlled: it could not conjure the 'involuntary memory' – which he believed to be the more powerful sort – that his famous madeleines dipped in tea could.

Yet I think orphan images are different. If, as discussed, they are freed from the constraints of our knowing about them, and therefore from being a snapshot of memory, designed to trigger something specific for their author or original owner, I wonder if they can then trigger the involuntary memories Proust held so highly, the sort that catch us unaware through unexpected associations. I look at the photos in this book and I think of my childhood, my pets and my grandmother. And each photo will have a different effect on each viewer.

Is art and creative interpretation where things can be immortalised differently to traditional monuments? I think of Gwen John again – leaving a legacy not just of her life but those of her cats, ensuring those she loved were remembered through her creativity. I think of the poems of the imagist Amy Lowell, especially an extract from her poem 'Chopin':

The cat and I
Together in the sultry night
Waited.
He greatly desired a mouse;
I, an idea.
Neither ambition was gratified.
So we watched
In a stiff and painful expectation.
Little breezes pattered among the trees,
And thin stars ticked at us
Faintly,
Exhausted pulses
Squeezing through mist.

Those others, I said!

The essence of her cat is there in the words on the page – a sense of personality and a real catness often lost in more clichéd descriptions. I believe that continuing to think creatively about something, to reassess and reimagine, is a way of ensuring a memory doesn't just become a concrete structure, an epitaph, or simply lost completely.

VIII How we record our lives has changed dramatically in my lifetime. From teenage diaries and beloved, unedited snaps, picked up from the photo developers when I'd been able to afford a film for a holiday, an exciting night out or party with friends, to digital cameras and phones and social media. I have virtually no photos of childhood pets; the images of my youth fit in a small box. Today people have hundreds. And the goal is different. Where in the past, personal photos were essentially a private matter for family and friends, today they are arguably a representation of one's life available to be viewed by strangers, a filter for them to see our lives through, where we curate how we want to be seen. People have always dressed up and posed for photos, but to impress family and people we know – not strangers. Yet this modernising of the relationship between memory and image has made it more disposable – we photograph and curate intensively yet delete with as much voracity. The flippancy of instant photography, the digital throwaway culture, lessens the specialness of the individual personal photograph.

Orphan images are in danger of extinction – such a project as this, in the future, may not be possible. Unwanted images having been deleted, those archived will remain attached to a specific human's profile – date stamps, location, time, tags, the data may be ignored but it will always be there somewhere. Photography as cherished object, as memory made paper, is ceasing to exist.

And yet, there has been a resurgence in Polaroids and teenagers using disposable cameras, maybe embracing this unedited experience of moment capturing, a harkening back to the past when their parents talk of going to shops to collect developed films, excited about what the photos might show. But this aside, photography is no longer a blind gamble, a moment of anticipation for what your printed memories might be, a moment of no control, an uncurated image, of something to be used sparingly due to cost.

But perhaps because of this there is now something more urgent in the archiving of everyday images in the form of physical photographs – not the grand portraits of historically significant moments, but the images of normal life and people and, in my mind, the pets. Unlike the thousands of digital photos we take today, these historical images could be lost – they are fragile. Yes computers crash, but most people back things up – there are records upon records. Orphan images are unique – rarely found with their negatives, there is no back up. Left to the wilds of the world, no owners to champion their preservation, it would be easy for them to disappear.

I remember as a child thinking deeply about how if no one remembers us and we are forgotten, do we cease to exist? Maybe we would still have a gravestone – but stone and an epitaph tell us nothing. And then pets – well, they rarely even have that. They lie in gardens and people's heads. Except for the few examples in books and the photos that are left behind.

I cannot know for sure, but I suspect that all the cats in the photos in this book and many of the women too are now forgotten, though some may still be remembered by younger friends and relations, or by something they may have created, and if so I would love to know. But if my book succeeds as an object of creative remembering, if it can create 'new memory' through the imagination of strangers, then these women and cats are alive in someone's heads; they are not forgotten. So my childhood worry is assuaged – they have not ceased to exist.

So I think back through my life with cats and my research. I think of adventures. I think of distant places – the street cats from my travels, the ladies who fed them. Rome, Tbilisi – I remember night time Istanbul was awash with cats. Holiday cats in France and Iceland. Friends' cats from childhood. I let my imagination drift back through history to the ordinary women accused of witchcraft – the semi-feral cats climbing through windows for scraps and warm fires.

I think of Dylan. I think of love and how he has turned to dust but the love is still real – the love is still there. It's just invisible to most.

I think not of the photos, but of the real women, girls and cats in them and how they felt about each other.

I make a pledge.

When I walk the streets from now on the pavements will be alive with memories. I picture them forming in the shape of pets, or being joined by them, but without the weight of bodies they can spin and fly without wings.

Dylan's old bones are no longer stiff and he is leaping from lamp posts to roofs to my shoulders. And then the cats in these photos join him. They peel their forms from the faded paper and become 3D, shake out their fur, stretch their legs and rusty claws. He shows them how to dance like Kate Bush and hunt seaweed, chase dogs and roam a territory as wide as oceans will allow. And they have a clowder ball – no cat fights, just dancing.

These cats and their women. They will no longer be lost.

They can have new stories – live again in people's imaginations where they can be memorialised. And my Dylan, he will be with them – reassure them that all will be OK. It was his superpower: the ability to create hope, to take pain away and in its place leave joy.

From goddesses to witches, false or true; from artists and writers to the women who do choose to live alone with 15 cats and have the right to do so; to the ordinary women and extraordinary feline friendships.

They are all Cat Women, and that is a thing to celebrate.

Where they're not taken from inscriptions, all names are created by the author.

Inscription on back: March 1964
Found in: USA

–

Woman with
Shadow Dancers

This picture is bathed in sun water. The cats are charming
the air, capturing the patterns of light to play with, spinning
these darkened visual echoes of trees. Jeanie perches in the door
of her caravan, knees and heels neatly together, her tidiness
a contrast to any preconceptions of her setting. I imagine
the concrete block she rests her toes on as a brutalist secret
passageway I almost expect more cats to shoot out of.

Tabby the cat stretches and the pole-shaped shadow
echoes his moves, as his cat friends, the white and black twins,
wreathe the other shadows like a maypole. Shadow folk dance!
With strange stretches! Is this their own tradition we can
know nothing of?

Yet Tabby's whole fur is shadows – a reverse of dappled
light that, when shed, is curiously black tipped and ginger at
the root. Oh, to have hair that colour naturally! she thinks.
Oh, for the power to manipulate the reflections of trees – the

wall is made river by them and the cats are tempted to pounce and pull and see what happens. If they can catch wall fish, if their claws can peel the shadows and trail them like ribbons of almost bark.

Jeanie smiles. This isn't the life that was expected for her, but she is content here, feeding titbits to her shadow cats, feeling sun patterns tickle and warm her face, making the cats dance, eyes intent on her and paws outstretched in an invitation to take the floor.

Her smile is secret and content. This is the best sort.

The HP cardboard box under her trailer is full of her shadows – she hides them there. The cats stay clear in reverence. But this is a good day, full of light.

Inscription on back: None
Era: c. 1930s–50s
Found in: USA

Girl on Step with Chubby Almost Tiger

The setting up of a small table for a child is ever so important – whether for an invisible tea party or as a special desk, it is an object of reverence she must gaze at and rest her hands upon. Georgie (Porgie pudding and pie) wants to join in, though would rather any tea party were not invisible as he is rather fond of snacks. He is a little rotund, though this playing outside keeps him in shape and no one wants a skinny cat.

The steps are golden and fall like a royal carpet would, away from the shadows and the strange giant moths or manta rays of light that fly or swim behind them. Georgie is not that interested, though seen alone they would render this photo magic. The veranda they move through is another realm – all dark and contained and somehow a different consistency of air or water to this bright sunshine, the bleached-out white of the little girl's step, where she sits with her cat and her table.

Georgie is kind, I think. An older gentleman, he has known her since birth and would do anything to protect her. Her parents know this so feel quite safe if she is outside and with him. They know that if she fell he would come trotting in to get help, or if she only needed him, not leave her side. He is a sensitive guard/doctor cat. The latter are a real thing, I think – some cats know when you are ill or need them. Come and sit in just the right place to soothe your pain.

He's had his own pain. It might be the angle, but his tail seems shorter than it should be – as if its end were lost to some long-ago danger. There is a strange pile of earth to one side, a shadow in its centre like the focus of a flower, a concrete daisy. I wonder if she took his lost tail and buried it there. Marked the spot with darkness. Kissed him better and made him some invisible tea.

Inscription on back: August Monday 7th,
1950, in our garden
Found in: UK

–

Two Women and
a Ginger Gem

This is a photo of wind not stillness – you can feel it – and
bright sun, bursting like an explosion of blinding powder paint,
scattering the ground beyond the wall so the grass is like glow
worms, if only we could see more of it. The large white stones –
born that way or spread with lichen butter – watch on like the
eyes of a wall monster. The two ladies do not see it, or maybe
he is their pet too and this whole garden is alive, but if not,
Charles, their fine ginger gem of a tom cat, knows they're there
– he can feel the stones watching curiously.

From the handwritten note on the back, we know that this photo was taken in these ladies' garden, but there is something slightly reminiscent of a rural cemetery – the path and railings, how it is slightly wild and gentle. I like cemeteries so I don't mean to say that it is a gothic place or a place of death, more that there is a sense of memory and age – a gentle reverence to this outdoor space they share between the three of them. They seem happy together, hinting at smiles – the lady on the left reminds me of my grandmother; the ginger tom reminds me of my childhood cat Sandy, who lived rather indifferently in our family for my first 19 years – my big brother was given him as a kitten to make up for my being born.

The breeze is catching wisps of hair and holding them like the smears of paint brushes. They are on the edge of wilderness here, though Charles is used to this fine line between domesticity and the wild. The fence protects them, almost, but he can come and go.

A flower rests on both their shoulders like embroidery, whereas Charles needs no ornament. His front legs are held neatly and, though clasped tightly, he is not trying to get away. They are all friends here – he keeps to himself but joins them for afternoon tea, a saucer of milk. He is not a stray, but rather chose to live with them. He just showed up one day, or perhaps was found as a kitten curled up and scared after his mother was killed by a fox. Either way, he is part of their little life here – wild, yet protected from the outside world.

The fronds of plants by their knees wave like seaweed. `

In the top left-hand corner there is a stone ghost in the shape that ghosts should be – made of sheets with holes for eyes. This place is alive. Charles waits patiently.

Inscription on back:
Mary with the V.I.C(at). 1955
Found in: UK

-

Mary and the V.I.C(at)

Many of us who were born in the seventies and eighties have a strange familiarity with the 1950s, absorbed from films or photos – or just from the style of our grannies who held on to their aesthetic from their late youth.

I can picture Mary, long after this photo was taken, older and watching telly, eating Quality Street like my granny Hazel did. She would have a cat on her lap, but thinking of this other cat, her dear friend she lost long ago. Her VIC – her Very Important Cat.

His fluffiness is a luxuriance, like a living stole stroking her neck and adding a little something to her simple sweater. It's probably not a coordinated approach – a conscious outfit decision – but the holding of him nevertheless adds something to her look. He drapes his paw across her shoulder, his tail at just the right angle, trailing past her waist. A living sash. She needs no brooch, no set of pearls. He turns and watches the camera as if knowing his beauty, the thick shine of his coat. His body is weighty and warm against hers, though I think it is a mild day. Weather can be hard to tell in black and white photos, but her sleeves are rolled up and the small glimpse of sky could just as well be blue as grey.

Cats can notoriously control the weather, but being a VIC is a time-consuming enough occupation without being bothered to call up storms. He prefers the sun as most cats do – it sets off his shine just right and warms him to the perfect temperature. So he stays there, showing himself off to his best advantage. Look at me and Mary, he says, we are one and at this angle, this framing of a moment; you can never pull us apart.

Inscription on back: Jan nineteenth 1949
Found in: USA

Lucy and Mittens

They have teleported – three tiers into a Rothko painting,
though more textured and full of cold. Time travellers.
Companions through space and time, to land here, to crouch,
confused. The footprints aren't going in the right direction for
them to have arrived in any other way.

Star-patterned gloves grip her tight. Mittens. She is so
small to be in the snow; her tail is almost reaching the ice.
The patterns which she has accidentally made around her
are star-shaped too.

Is there a shadow dog hiding here? I had looked at this photo
many times before I began to wonder and I cannot be sure. In
folklore, black dogs are often sinister, though there is one in
Somerset who roams the hills to protect lost children . . .

A determination – we will crouch and withstand the snow!
The war is nearly five years gone now, though I wonder at that
wooden cross, at what it means. A grave? Its scale is hard to tell
and the frosted brambles are knotted swathes of barbed wire.
Three horizontal lines: sky, tangled blades and snow. Just a girl
and a cat, a maybe-dog, and a cross, interrupting.

Wisps of distant trees – smudged hair between brambles and sky. Girl looks less comfy than cat, despite the strange gloved gripping. Iced breath light. Lucy, Lucy, you shall hold Mittens tight.

I think of abandoned prison camps.

I wonder who knitted those stars. Whose feet and paws patterned the ground? Or are the indents just echoes of something soft and dark and long ago . . .

Inscription on back: None
Era: c. 1920s-30s
Found in: Europe

Family Portrait

A mother sits, her daughter stands, made one by the curve of an arm. The cat has been grabbed to make a triptych – their little family – a tumble of curves. Though he has not quite made it to mother's lap, so while she smiles he is somewhat glaring. The indignity of being held like this! He is superb at balancing and sitting on laps looking handsome! What a record for posterity – that his skills should not be captured thus!

Yet despite this clumsiness, the warmth of this unit shines through, their smiles are so genuine. Her two children – daughter in one arm, cat in the other. The love is there for all to see.

The garden behind them is awash with plants – a herbaceous border, dense and wild, supports them like the back of a giant natural armchair.

Just for a moment, let's close our eyes and see him as he wants to be seen: sitting proudly upright, thick silver fur groomed to perfection, a handsome gaze, dignified and wise for eternity.

Inscription on back: Rosalind 1930
Found in: UK

‒

Rosalind the Nursemaid

Tabby markings swirl like ink marbling, swaddling his chubby form. Rosalind lifts Marmalade out of the pram – her precious patient. They have been playing all morning. He sat so well in the pram and, although a bit bewildered by the movement of the wheels, had not leapt out, even when a leaf blew by like a crunchy moth or butterfly. He could sense that this was important to her. So he sat and groomed his white bib.

And now, paw placed protectively in the crook of Rosalind's elbow, he waits as she poses for the camera. They stand in sharp focus, compared to the damp, not-quite-mud of the garden behind them. Her grey ribbed tights and sensible shoes are not bad, but not perfect for this weather. They are a strange clash with the whiteness of her uniform and the sleekness of his fur.

Marmalade is not sure what to do – should he move yet? When is it OK to jump down? He quite wants to investigate what is going on in the plants behind them, but he does not want to disappoint her – she is his best friend after all.

Some days, as she wheels him or lifts him gently, he catches glimpses of a world beyond theirs, a world beyond the walls of this garden. Birds take off from branches and leave via the sky, squirrels climb away – he can smell and hear things he cannot see here. But he will not go and investigate, he is too loyal. For all his remaining days he will not leave her. When you truly love another creature it is hard to be free.

Inscription on back: None
Era: c. 1940s-50s
Found in: USA

Maude and Pipsqueak

What a strange array of sticks, Pipsqueak thinks, seeing the steps and raised area complete with deckchair, outside of their mobile home. The angles make it seem like a sculpture or a weird wooden robot. The vase of faded flowers is a gentle attempt at adding some softness to its lines. The home has wheels too – like an old railway carriage to carry them away on any flights of fancy.

Maude looks happy, content with their little mobile realm. I wonder how Pipsqueak would feel if they really travelled though – cats are so territorial that leaving the confines of their small home could be traumatic. Or perhaps she is one of the few traveller cats, the cat with no territory, the cat that can conquer any new terrain with gusto like a dog, the cat that can let go of past lives (as long as they don't move more than nine times) and ramble away onwards into an ever-changing landscape. Sometimes on my walks I see canal cats, they must

move lots and they seem OK – the roof of their narrowboat and the towpath one endless domain.

Maude sits and holds her tight, though she is sliding off. She wears a sensible matching top and trousers; the roots of Maude's hair show their grey, but the pearls add a certain decadence. Her right fingers tickle Pipsqueak's foot, as if to make up for the incompetence of her left arm's grasp.

There is a thread of light, spilling a footpath on the ground beneath them – maybe she should follow that, Pipsqueak thinks. Maybe it would lead to a magical forest full of sun-coloured birds and glittering mice. It would be brighter than where she is now. The faded curtains and thin wooden walls, the uneven windows looking wistfully out, on to a world that's not moving.

Inscription on back: None
Era: c. 1930s-40s
Found in: UK/Northern Europe

—

Girl with Siamese

The background is verdant and soft, but the face that stares
out is a strong one, reminiscent of that famous Walker Evans
portrait of Allie Mae Burroughs in Depression-era America. It
could almost be her, except for the lush green and the cardigan,
the paler hair to match her Siamese cat, the slight petulance in
her stare.

I wonder if there is a different sort of depression here,
one not of economic but internal worry, or whether I am
putting on this image my own associations – thinking too of
Dorothea Lange and her images such as *Migrant Mother* of 1936.
This is just a young woman, in a plain cotton dress and sensible
cardigan, in an overgrown garden, holding her cat possessively.

Was someone trying to take it away? Did they disapprove of
the weight she gave this creature? The sides of the photo have
been trimmed and I wonder what or who was cut out. The ivy
is taking over the wall like heart-shaped fur, and is crawling
towards them, forming the skin of a new creature. But I don't
feel it is sinister.

Sadie the Siamese cat is not looking behind her, but just
off to the side. Something is coming, but the young woman is
defiant, standing her ground against whatever it might be.

The swirl inside her and the invisible ribbons that bind her
and Sadie are stronger than any threat. She will not leave her,
she will not care.

Inscription on back: None
Era: c. 1940s
Found in: UK

–

Two Ladies
with Kitten

It's funny how people cradle human babies but kittens are held up, paws in the mimic of a wave, a distinctly human action that cats would never do. These two ladies look very pleased though, framed by trees on a summer lawn. The purpose of this photo is for them to show him off – to showcase him, not each other.

Yet they seem almost joined, these women – a friendship of non-identical conjoined twins, shoulder to shoulder. The woman in her best floral dress, with a lovely twist to the fabric of its waist, almost seems to have one arm missing, as if it has been absorbed into her friend who is on kitten-showing duty.

Friends or sisters? They make me think of my granny and her best friend who, after the First World War, thought they'd never marry, then two brothers came along and they both had children in their forties – unusual for those days. But I still picture them together. I could see them in another world, living together like this with their cat baby in their beautiful garden. Making an effort with their clothes for the camera, wearing matching sensible shoes for walking on grass.

The bond of woman and cat is hard to know about here – it is all about the future. What might this kitten bring to them? There was a whole cat life after this image was taken. He grew in his black and whiteness and prowled this lawn and those trees for years. He looked after them as they got older, nursing them through, till he, maybe 18 years on, needed nursing too. Then, as an old man, he lay down in the garden at the end of his happy, long life, and left on his own adventure.

Inscription on back: None
Era: c. 1950s-60s
Found in: UK

Softly Now,
Sweet Jimmy

The streets are blurred – has someone left her, and her pain
in this moment has made the air lose focus? Yet despite the
heartbreak she still has Jimmy and his black and white fur.
She holds his tail tight, not to hurt him, but to keep him close
to her, to protect him from the grey shades of a world that
could be so cruel. He protects her, too – does so every day, if
only she knew it. He watches out for dogs. Scratches people he
disapproves of.

Her watch is a shackle – too high and digging in. Jimmy
would give her gypsy bracelets to jangle and dance with –
decorate her and set her free to twirl down the street like a
spinning top, swishing skirts and tinkling bells. He would join
her and play with them. Summon a kind tornado – he could
do that, if the legends are to be believed. Her hair blurs into a
smudge. She has forgotten to brush it and she does not care,
and why should she?

Come get us life foes – we can defeat you! We have imaginary
swords smelt from love!

There are some pains only cats can head-nudge and make
better.

The street aches with her stories, it is almost trembling with
their vibrations, but in all this Jimmy holds still.

Inscription on back: Aug 1944
Found in: USA
-

Anne (with an e)
and Cowslip

They are on the cusp, both not quite children, but being a
grown up seems so distant, so far away. Anne looks gently at
Cowslip as she tentatively explores the bench. The kitten is a
little nervous – perhaps this is her first time outside. They are
both shy, but not of each other. There is an understanding that
passes most (not all) adults by.

Gentle curve of shoulders, hands not held out just yet – she
will come to you, with patience.

Both hair and fur catch gold from the sky as the lawn
shimmers. Deckchair or mint humbug stripes and lace – the
sun is greedy for decoration today. But the beauty of the
accident of light around her is nothing compared to Anne's
love and understanding for this little cat, this nervous
sweetheart. Come here my darling, the rest of the world
can sparkle then fade away.

Inscription on back: December 1955
Found in: USA

Retro-futurism

Standing still, trying not to slip on snow, she shows off her new haircut, and how he can perch on her shoulder, parrot-like and fluffy in the cold. Together their heads make a perfect V to suit the angles of the time.

She checks in with him. Is this quite all right? He is unsure. He's not keen on this white stuff that coats the ground – it is too cold on his paws and he does not have all her extra layers. Her cocoon of a long wool coat.

They are a future that never happened – space-age cars, even the snow carves the roof to the shape of curved fins and imaginary spaceships. The car has eyes and looks like it should be in an old hand-drawn advertisement for the lifestyle you always wanted. Ice-blue paint and old metal curves.

Fashions change, but cats are constant – hundreds of years ago they would have looked the same, while we are defined by the age we are born to.

She smiles. They feel magic together. But not magic of the old kind, just the sort that makes a freezing day feel warm inside. The soft miracle of curled up fur. The perfect timeless companion to her modern architecture.

Inscription on back: None
Era: c. 1920s
Found in: France

Gingham Twins

The tree is an endless pole, stretching upwards to heights
the kittens cannot yet imagine. A beanstalk. A ship's mast
for mythical crow's nests.

Her eyes are closed, the camera catching the moment our
eyes rarely do: the imperceptibility of blinking. She smiles.
Her thick hair is pulled back with grips; her gingham apron
covers the pattern of her good dress. Her hand reaches one
kitten and strokes his cheek, but his sister raises her head in
tickled bliss as if there is an extra, invisible hand, friendly ghost
fingers, stroking her too. Gemini kittens.

I know where I found this photo but not what country it
was taken in. It feels Near Eastern to me – Turkey maybe . . .
Southeast Europe?

There is a shadow at the bottom that looks like the echo
of water poured away – the remnants of a magical route the
kittens arrived on perhaps, floating in on boats made of leaves,
to stop at this strange tall pole and gaze up. She wants to
be close to them, but they seem otherworldly, like mythical
creatures. Kitten oracles. There are rusty buckets lying as if
receptacles to catch their pronouncements on her dreams.
She has not lost all of those yet, crouching in her garden,
her hems dusting the ground. She is smiling for the kittens'
wonder; for their foretelling – a glimpse of what could be.

Back yard   1921

–

Teenage Dreaming

He's wrapped in arms; she frames him, a tender representation
of perfect teenage dreaminess, when the world is vast and
full and for the taking. But here, it is a smaller world – her
backyard, garden, their special place to sit in sun – a microcosm
of freedom on long-drawn summer days, when shoes get lost
and hairbrushes are discarded to fly through the air like clumsy
dragonflies. They only need the sun and each other. The ground
is hard and dry, with scrubby green, like the bird's-eye view
of a desert. They are giants in this landscape and the rain has
decided to hibernate, which is good for the cat who does not
care for getting wet. He loves her arms though. Just sitting
there together. Her bare feet outstretched, her simple cotton
dress. If she leaves the house she's forced to change – shoes and
stockings and unnecessary grooming – while he is left behind
to pine for her, to watch her through the window or wooden
gate as she disappears from view, not looking like her true self.

In a few years she might leave him to go out dancing –
sequins all a flutter of flapper fringes. Not yet, he thinks,
hunkering down in her flesh cradle.

The glow of the frame looks like a portal, opening or closing
on this snapshot in time. If this were a portal, she would
happily stay frozen in this moment. Dreaming of a life of
adventure, but sitting still, with her best friend, in her most
perfect moment in the whole wide world.

She holds him protectively as their edges blur. The cat smiles
and settles down as she strokes him.

Inscription on back: None
Era: c. 1950s
Found in: USA

–

Christmas Cat

'Tis a special season when the tree rival comes indoors.
This is not their first Christmas together, and each year they
pose together by the sparkling tree, real candles floating, a fire
hazard from a different time.

Phyllis has a tendency to go dreamy this time of year and
Tinsel has to be vigilant, to make sure that it eventually goes
back to normal. The house becomes full of boxes and there is
shiny paper to play with, only not to the point where there is
no time for cuddles. Tinsel doesn't like too many others around.

Almond eyes, white chubbiness and distinct black splodges
between her ears, she watches us, calm and thoughtful – a look-
afterer cat. Phyllis, holding her tight, can never be sad with her
in her arms. Tinsel knows how to fill a room with the spirit of
this season even in summertime.

A Christmas pudding bauble hovers, standing out where
other baubles are almost camouflaged. Did they decorate
this tree together? Tinsel helpfully pulling at the glittering
threads with her paws, knocking the tree to a certain angle?
They are proud of this tree and each other. Tinsel's greatest
achievements: her love for Phyllis and tolerance of this
temporary prickly rival creature that never moves lest pushed.

It's a good game, this time of year, but she'll be quite pleased
come Epiphany when she has Phyllis all to herself again.

Inscription on back: None
Era: c. 1920s
Found in: Northern Europe

Λ Furry Bundle
for Zelda

It is easy to miss the second cat; he disappears into the white
of her floral dress, or maybe fades next to the tabby stripes of
his friend, though his black headband stands out, an accidental
fashion statement. The cats must be friends or she could never
hold so still, her body so calm, arms soft and devoid of all
scratches. I can picture them at home, curled up on the sofa –
the joy of being able to cuddle them both so close as if living
toys, cat teddy bears all kind and patient despite odd angles and
elbows and the occasional precariously balanced book. She likes
to read on languid nights – smoky tea in thin china.

The sun makes a scalloped necklace of shade around her
collarbone, her eyes framed by natural sunglasses of shadow.
The tree waves its branches like chubby fingers above the blur
of wall and ground.

She manages the challenge of holding two cats well. A tumble
of squidgy fur, eyes half shut and paws dangling, they notice
nobody but each other. But her gaze is different, her knowing
smile: slightly incredulous, she notices everything.

Inscription on back: None
Era: c. 1910s
Found in: UK

–

Emmeline
and Spark

Edwardian or just after, I think – crisp white cotton of nurses or household work. A cat nurse? The first female vet was not recognised till 1922. Her hair is piled and she is spotless, but there is no primness to her joy. Spark is young – blackest fur defying the inherent darkness of its associations: he is a bright spark.

This is a garden, but somehow the upright poles of the background make me think of bulrushes. Spark has seen something and twists his small head away from the camera as Emmeline grins towards us.

She tickles under his chin gently. They are new-found friends, I think, and she is so pleased to have him. Vines grow – the whole background is growing taller – but she is just concerned with Spark. Her arms rest on the path as if its background stripe were a support to help her keep Spark upright, looking out, all meerkat and curious in his youth. Their monochrome of black cat and white uniform makes the black and white of the rest of the photo almost show its green.

Summer. A young cat. This photo is a portrait of beginnings.

Inscription on back: None
Era: c. 1940s
Found in: UK

The Ghost Watches

There is a ghost in the window: a puff of albino squid-ink smoke, hovering. Cat or human, I am not sure. The woman doesn't seem concerned, but there is a distinct worry in the little eyes of Pickle. It is too close and she is holding him firmly.

The bricks are slotted together like one of those plastic puzzles, but with a hint of liquorice allsorts – a fragment of the jigsaw that is the back of the buildings of this anonymous English city. On her dress, a purposeful detail near her shoulder that could be a tear from naughty claws and teeth. His tail thick from either natural luxuriance or fear – his hair stands on end to show him at his fullest ferocity.

They too could be ghosts now, if ghosts exist. It's strange to think that. They are no more. Do pets wander the streets, continuing to guard their territory after death? Territory is very important to cats and they are loath to leave it. Do they stay with us? Happy and still at home, watching out of windows as the world passes by, keeping an eye on us all so we are never alone?

The softness of fur is a comfort.

Inscription on back: None
Era: c. 1900s–1910s
Found in: Germany

–

A Potential
Fairy Tale

The gaze of a tiger, so direct, is strange in one so small.
Only her head above hands, but she is watching us, not the
photographer who Solveig, the young woman, looks at, stands
straight for, and slightly parts her mouth.

We are somewhere in Eastern Europe, perhaps within the
Austro-Hungarian Empire. The clothes suggest that it is before
both world wars – a different world not scarred in the way it
soon will be. So they stand in a lost world that no one still alive
can remember.

The kitten she holds is Gretel; her brother Hansel is
elsewhere, a black blur battling the wire fence, with its
honeycomb-shaped traps for tiny paws. He is a strange
contrast to the composed stare of Gretel – all movement,
his tail flicks the photo into distortion; he is a curious rebel,
a trait I hope will not lead him into trouble.

Solveig's mother sweeps round small enamel bowls for water,
her arms a blur made ghost-like by the combination of camera
and movement. A chamber pot has been repurposed for plants.
Shutters on the outside of windows are another visual clue
that says 'not England' – though they make good climbing
swings for kittens.

Were Hansel and Gretel lost in the woods, strays to whom
Solveig gave a home, or bred from a much-loved family pet?
She holds Gretel as if she knows she is a special creature, but
Hansel is left to the obstacles of the wild.

Later, though, they will come indoors, curl up together
in a small basket near a fire and sleep blissfully, as kittens
do, dream of a future, the real version of which none of
them could imagine.

Inscription on the back. Remember my
white kitty on farm [word illegible] on
front porch out there
Era: c. 1940s
Found in: USA

White Kitty of the Lost Farm

No name – just *my white kitty*. The call to remember makes me think I was supposed to find this photo – that this was a bond she did not want forgotten, formed with a special animal. Eyes closed, she is smiling, but it is the love for her cat that stands out. I recognise this joy that almost borders on sadness – it is bound up with the knowledge that this relationship might be fleeting, that unlike our children the chances are we outlive our pets.

She cuddles him properly. The sun obscures his features, bleaches out the details that made his face unique, but we can see how his head rests on her – the contentment. Their love is in a natural spotlight. He cuddles her too.

The brick behind her looks new – a modern farmhouse perhaps, but I can sense the warmth of an old building. Generations of wellies and a couple of crumbling barns; farm cats run around, making nests of straw and feasting on rats and mice, teaching their kittens as cows munch steadily. For this woman and her white kitty, this is a photo of home.

Inscription on back: None
Era: c. 1940s–50s
Found in: USA, but possibly
taken elsewhere

Mother and
Daughter

Sun and leaf smudges on whitewashed walls. Despite the
mother's smart wool suit, this photo sings of the Mediterranean
or Latin America. The bleached-out warmth of the light is
wrong for anywhere else.

Darker leaves drip chandeliers as the daughter gazes down at
her kitten. A white cotton cloth drapes her sleeve like the train
of a christening gown, there to show off her beautiful creature.
Her smart heels and beads and her styled hair show the
importance of the occasion, yet her lovely clothes are folksy in
style – tiers and embroidered ribbon; gathers and full sleeves.
They have a formal freedom next to the suit and pussybow
collar of her mother's blouse.

I almost feel as if they are taking the kitten to church. There
is a reverence to this image that contrasts with the laid-back
summer light, the slower pace, the scent of herbs and tomatoes,
crickets singing in the long, dry nearby grass.

Oh, the joy of being admired. As she grows she will
understand better than most do, for cats love to be admired.
She will learn how to preen her fur just right for the occasion,
to dress herself to her best advantage, to gaze out and absorb
the looks of wonder.

On this perfect day of warmth, all three of them have risen
to the occasion.

Inscription on back: None
Era: c. 1920s
Found in: UK

-

Soot and Jennifer

The building breathes shadows. Soot curls into her owner,
Jennifer, like a silhouette, a shape almost not cat, but for the
inquisitively pointing ear. I think she knows about shadows –
the secrets that can be held in tricks of light.

Jennifer is in focus and her feet are like reflections; the
ground a misty pool of water, the feelings of her defiant elbow
seeping into the background. Chin on fist, Jennifer stares out.
Weighted brows, a mouth that could be about to open:
a protest or just incredulous – it is hard to tell.

A lost flower ghost or paper bird hovers on the ground –
Soot's enchanted treat instead of mice. Soot watches intently
as the leaves blur into outlines of islands, places she will never
go. The large fence is as a frame for this inaction, a barrier.

Is a gap in the wall a tunnel to light, or a sheet hanging on a
washing line? The branches of the trees are a black cloud; the
leaves are only perceptible at the edges, otherwise all is solid
lack of light.

I wonder if this is a home or a hospital and then I wish my
brain did not so easily go there. Jennifer might be happy, feeling
calm and balanced. Surely Soot would make her a little happy –
cats are the best therapists, they do not ask questions.

I wonder if she is really there, or if this background is her
imagination made real, its colour scheme and blurred edges
projected on a blank screen so she can escape them.

Soot licks her paws as the building rumbles.

Inscription on back: None
Era: c. 1930s–40s
Found in: USA

The Explorers

Thin tail, paws to the sky and a little shyness. He waits patiently as she holds up his paws for the camera. Even at this young age he has his suspicions that older cats might tease and say this is a little undignified, and that really his paws should be washing his face or spiking a nice fresh mouse with his claws. But he loves her and she wants this photo. What the other cats don't realise is that this silly pose isn't the end, but rather the beginning of an adventure, and if there is anything cats are very good at it is adventures.

They are both young here, both kittens. Her few years don't add up to much more than his few months. Two sides to this photo – a bright burst of light to one side, a straight dark door to the other. Two choices: Narnia-like adventure or the comfort of home.

Not to worry though – she seems to have him safe and he's not wriggling. A prized possession! No photo must be taken without him! He is her companion after all and this is their moment. The moment before they set off – the beginning of all expeditions – should be captured on film as they may not return home the same.

Sensible shoes laced tight, trousers – no frilly dress here.
A bonnet yes, but the tropical sun that might lie beyond any
portal would need that. Footpaths are no match for them when
cameras are gone and they stride out as if through jungles. She
a lady explorer, he her trusted tiger pal.

Young, like she is, he stares out, unsure, the camera but
another object in their now vast world, laid out all panoramic
for the conquering.

Inscription on backs: None
Era: c. 1900s
Found in: UK

-

An Edwardian
Photo Story

He appeared one day – a teleportation of fluff direct to the perfect cushion they had laid out, should such an occasion ever occur. He waited patiently for his splendour to be noticed.

Then he grew. Outside now. A ring of white stones, house teeth, smile and wait for the moment he will understand the gestures – that it is her hand, not her skirt, that he should follow.

Bay window eyes glint – laugh in their open crow's-feet corners. The ball is a good choice. Almost prey. The white chair has come out to watch as she sits on the grass to encourage him. She has stolen his cushion.

Tent creature, tree and deckchair. All are curious. Her hand is dangling something and he looks up. Almost ready to jump, he has not noticed the ghost thumbprint in the corner – the cut-out door in the tent just right for mythical creatures or a sudden explosion of breath.

He is a wonder of meaningful indifference. Still she tries – a new chair, a different piece of string, but the wrong cushion. He looks away. A piece of netting on the ground is more fascinating in its disembodied randomness. The strange gnarled bench under the tree has a gravel tongue. This garden is alive with things she hasn't realised.

A new tent creature slowly moves around the garden flanked by a loyal herd of empty chairs. They are all gathering, watching on, but still he stares out, indifferent to her circus trick aspirations. The tent creature's draped mouth is devouring the chairs.

Even this does not move the cat. He has the power here and stares down the camera accordingly. Something's changed. Tent mouth open, some chairs have escaped . . . He looks back, slightly wary. Tail unsure. Yet still she stands as if simply trying enough times will make him do it.

A fine pram contraption joins them now, with spindly penny farthing-like wheels. His life has changed since this child emerged. He makes his escape, those chubby hands too close for comfort. This was not his plan for them once she had stopped the whole trick training thing. A once-fine chair is piled high with stuff – substandard cushions and collapsed bunting. The gazebo-type structure with edges like Pacman ghosts gives the air of an abandoned garden party after a storm.

She is on his cushion. He gives her his best aggrieved stare, but still, he is kind. Sits with her for the camera. He would never let her come to harm. He is used to her and the extravagant frills of her bonnet are to his liking.

Older now. Back to the house and its stone teeth. Finally his cushion has been placed beneath him. Just for him. Now she understands he needs his silken throne, his window and his solitude, she raises her hand and his front paws lift. Years later, in just his right circumstances, he is performing for the camera.

Inscription on back: (printed) Kodacolor
Nov 1963
Found in: UK

The Lost Summer
of Hazel

Suburbia. The words on the back are not handwritten but printed by the photo shop – 'Kodacolor Nov 1963'. But this is a photo of the heat of summer, and maybe the film got left in a drawer. Back then, you could forget things happened, find a film and develop it to bring back memories. She could have forgotten the strength of the bond she had with her cat, then suddenly be flooded with the memory of her months or years later.

Hazel the cat stares out – not at the camera, but across the all-green garden, distant and thoughtful. This photo is as much about what is not in it as what is. What does Hazel see? A bird perhaps, a floating leaf, a large mote of fluff, the wind made visible by how it blows through branches? It could be something too small for her owner to notice. She stands and smiles, all taken up with the showing off of her beloved stripy pet.

One support sock suggests her ankle is not quite right, but still it is summer and sandals must be worn – the sort only worn by older ladies even now. Her wrist is clasped by a cuff of gleaming metal fit for Wonder Woman. Maybe Hazel is her secret power? One flick of the tail against the cuff and a beam of light shoots out.

Hazel seems comfortable in her owner's arms, her fluffy tummy on display, balancing herself with front legs out across her owner's collar in a proprietary gesture. Her tail dips down as if testing the temperature of water that is not there. Daisies sprinkle the ground as if painted where Hazel's paws have pounced and danced.

Looking at this image I feel nostalgic for an era I was never in.

Inscription on back: August 1954
Found in: UK

-

Ring! Ring!

But, oh, for the sheer joy of a toy telephone! I remember that as a girl I had a Fisher Price one on wheels with wobbling eyes that I pulled on a lead like a pet. It gurgled in its own plastic way. But real pets are best, cats most of all, and she has one here – half her size and wearing the finest natural white bib and spats over his glossy, chubby blackness.

Her toes seem prepared for ballet in their dainty pointing. White Mary Janes – their feet match! His and hers white shoes! Though she does rather envy his paws and how far they let him leap. His claws and how he can scratch with them, legitimately, when cross. He is about to take off in this moment – he can see something ripe for the pouncing upon.

There is a strange contrast between the joy and the jumping and the concrete bareness of the back step they perch on. Girl and cat are all the life of this photo – her happiness so bright it distracts the eye from the rest. This place is glowing though it is the most ordinary, uninteresting location. The true 'place' here is that made between the girl, her toy phone and her cat.

I wonder if, in later years, she will fully embrace the Cat Lady, whose roots dug in like her friend's thin soft claws. Will she celebrate cats on biscuit tins and tea towels in her middle age, and not feel too bad when fatter and a little furrier.

Back then she had never wanted their adventure to end.

Inscription on back: Sammy and [word that looks like] Self, May, 1948
Found in: UK

-

The Frozen Tiers

We know, then, that he is Sammy: black on top and white below but for one black stripe under his chin, a bruise of molasses or fur treacle. But the lady stares out at us with no name, just the word *Self,* and perhaps a clue in the way she swirls her pen.

The wall behind her is remarkably neat. The brick, like a thick pie crust, leading down to a denser base of large pale stone that seems almost fake. A paler brick slope below that at last shows a little flaw – a bulge. It is as if she is in front of a stage set – a place that just does not look quite right.

The grass is thick but somehow seems bare. There is no life in this background. She seems so still, even for a photograph. Her face is smiling, but something seems frozen, though maybe she did not want to make Sammy jump off by moving suddenly. For he is certainly the main source of life here, the coiled energy I can imagine suddenly taking off and scampering up the slope on cat business. His front paws are in rest mode, neatly curling over her knee, and her left hand holds him back, but still I can see how easily he could leap away. Theirs is a friendship of choice – though of course most cat friendships are dependent on the cat's consent.

There is a country practicality to her good tweed and knitted sweater, the smart yet still sturdy shoes, that makes her seem too soft around the edges for this wall. I feel they should be in a cottage, in a village, or at least a 1930s house with a circular doorway and bay windows. There is no domesticity, no house here. A set. Not a place but a background. But Sammy knows what's out there. Sammy knows it all.

Inscription on back:
Morecambe, June 1956
Found in: UK

The Cat that is
Almost There

I think she believes he is next to her, but Boots is off, leaving
the frame so that on first glance this is simply a photo of a
woman alone in a garden. Her skirt drapes elegantly; if made in
silk and wearing a smarter top, she would look more at home at
a cocktail party than here in this garden.

It is a strange garden, on close inspection. Beyond its
overgrown wall there is a mysterious wasteland, and a fence
on top of a bare bank, beyond which could be anything: there
could be a beach – the writing on the back says Morecambe
after all – but it could just as easily be a prison or desert if we
take away that knowledge.

Apart from the concrete she sits on, however, her garden is
verdant, albeit slightly taken over by the strange plants at her
shoulders: a miniature city of floral futuristic skyscrapers
looming towards her, watching, waiting for their moment.

Boots is an older cat. He has that slightly less groomed and glossy look, the hint of grey in the black parts of his fur. I do not know if she is his true owner, whether they are close or his heart lies elsewhere. I wonder if he is a beach cat, whether he knows the quicksands and infamous tides of Morecambe Bay, whether he guides those who are lost, joins those out collecting cockles. Maybe he does love her, but after all these years of being a sea cat he is not concerned so much with the cut of a skirt, but the flounces of waves, the cool salt of the sea and the iodine tang of its flora.

The scent of vinegar and greased paper kisses the wind as he leaves her.

Inscription on back:
Mom with Suzy, July 1946.
Found in: USA

-

Proud Mom

Pure love to be holding her. Lush summer and sun swirls.
Suzy is debating making a break for it as she would much
rather be prowling the undergrowth like the mini tiger that
she is. But this is a family portrait, Mom's child taking the
shot, home in the garden with the warmth and the plants.
Mom holds her firmly – strong arms to match strong face and
sturdy clothes, a thick skirt even in this weather, though her
blouse is thin, summery with a fragile bow.

Suzy looks quite young and she's not a large cat. Slim and
stripy, her tail flicks in indecision as to how long she must
stay like this. Would it be a good launch height from which to
surprise some unsuspecting bird, or is her cover blown, shown
off like this for all the garden wildlife to see? One shoulder
is tucked behind a plant; they could be emerging from the
undergrowth, though normally Mom is not the best hunting
companion, rather overly fond of the smaller creatures
that live there.

The sun is shimmering with Mom's joy – she is radiating
the warmth of her family till it blurs the leaves, making the
air around her hazy. Natural happiness is so hard to capture
– smiles in photos are so often forced. But no 'cheese' was said
here, no pushing down of secret worry. Her garden is one joy,
but Suzy is so much more.

Inscription on back: None
Era: c. 1940s–50s
Found in: USA

Roly and Clare

Patiently he stares, fine tummy on display. Roly is almost as
big as Clare and quite a bit older. And he is not particularly
fond of tricycles, it has to be said. Or sitting upright like a
human. Moving on wheels. Being held tight. Yet here he is –
not wriggling or trying to get away – staring into space as
if wishing it were over, but nevertheless playing along for Clare.

Clare gazes up and looks a little grumpy, as if the grown-up
taking the photo has said something she disapproves of.
They do so often disapprove, grown-ups, seeming to think
she should be more ladylike and he should be left to be more
cat-like (Roly does slightly agree with the latter).

A white patch under his right ear is as a tag, so he can
always be identified. Lost, she would find him. And while the
recapture might be a little on the overly loving side, better to
be gently mauled than abandoned. There are real street cats
round here and he is sorry for them. At least Clare loves him.
However uncomfortable, he goes everywhere with her.

Flowers hover in the background like butterflies, captured by
branches. They are trapped till they fall as petals. Clare could
one day roam the world.

Inscription on back: None
Era: c. 1950s
Found in: UK

–

The Cat Obscurus

Such a sunny day. His owner has not seen it, but Fudge is all too aware of the shadow creature, a natural threat of summer, that moves around the deckchair. It wants to be part of her like he is – it joins her toes at the soles of her fluffy slippers (a curious choice of footwear for the garden) and steals all the sun in its attempt to consume them. The umbrella looms like a stiffened jellyfish and only aids the shadow creature. Fudge is very wary – if she would just let him go he would run away, or at least be able to give it a swipe to test the ferocity of this enemy, but she has him under his paws and, while a little uncomfortable, he does not like to upset her.

The little greenhouse watches on.

Fudge wishes his tummy wasn't on such display – it makes him vulnerable. Cats only reveal their tummies to most trusted friends and this creature of darkness is not that. He does not know what it is. Hold me tight, he thinks. If you will not let me go, hold me near.

Inscription on back: None
Era: c. 1920s–50s
Found in: USA

Girl with Bow

The bow is quite extraordinary. One could almost forget the girl and the cat for how it sits like a butterfly or giant tissue sweet wrapper, all scrunched and twisted as the ultimate in decoration. Who needs hair with such a bow? It is a visual distraction from the real object of her affection below: a fleeting filter, a kite fluttering before revealing what is behind it. The real life in this photo is the girl and her cat. The rest is kept behind the fence.

He has extremely luxuriant whiskers, though he's a skinny old thing. But he's well-loved and patient with young children, as so many lovely old animals are. He would never scratch no matter how annoying she was. He is just glad she doesn't make him wear the bow on this, the day of their great adventure.

Her hand rests gently on his silken stripes. A reassurance as much as to keep him there. We've done it! The fence is behind. She is smiling but her ear seems a little shy. He is not sure what to do, but there is no attempt to run away – he is flattened out not crouching. He is wary of leaving his territory as all cats are, so she has to be brave enough for both of them. He will always support her though. He is the elder and must look after his charge.

She is off centre. He is the centre here as if the photographer can sense his responsibility – the importance of keeping her joy safe. If you start your looking not with her, but him, the whole photo seems to shift. The houses a heavy bundle where sky should be, the grass a framing blanket.

They are in front. Free now from the world in the background, they have escaped the constraints of this distant urban childhood.

Inscription on back: None
Era: c. 1930s-40s
Found in: UK

Celia and Stripe

He's going doolally, blissed out as she holds him so protectively, his front paw floppy as it would be relaxed on the bed at home. Head tilted, his nose is a thin white stripe as if paint stroked on with fingers. His closed eyes are white too – when open does he have spectacles? Panda bear cat. His paws are a little grubby from exploring dusty ground. Whiskers so bright I can even see them in front of the pale skin of her fingers.

Flowers peer over the wall, defined as if outlined in pen, a living wreath of petal eyes gorging on the snuggling. More eyes look out below from the pattern in the grain of the wood that makes their planters.

The subtle godets of her hem suggest the 1930s, but it could be a few years either side – there's no date marked, no names. Just her casual lean, his happiness, her gaze a little whimsical, a touch of humour in an almost smile. I do not know where they are. The architecture gives nothing concrete away. The concrete gives nothing but patterns and a resting place for scattered light.

Inscription on back: None
Era: c. 1950s
Found in: UK

Backdoor Resting

Cradling the loose end of a washing line she rests. A well-earned sit on the steps and a bowl of food for the cat. Something hides behind the drainpipe – a secret package? A bag and perhaps a stove can be seen just inside the door, but summer is for outside, a magic time when clothes dry in the air. (A curious display, he thinks; why do they not wear all their fur but hang some of it up for all to see, blowing in the wind, obscuring some of this glorious warm light?)

The line is tied, where once broken, and the frayed ends look like a bird has been caught mid-air and is hanging by its beak. The cat can tell the difference, though still, it would be a good leaping challenge (after dinner that is).

She smiles. She is tired, but content. The most remarkable thing about this photo is somehow its encapsulation of absolute normalness. There is nothing unusual here but the clues we make for ourselves as viewers, the signifiers, the way we notice what we would normally miss: two black stripes at the top of the tiles, the subtle shades of bricks, a pole or air vent, a smudge of shadow or a grandiose weed pushing proudly with plant wings out of the grass.

It is the tiniest moment in history . . . yet preserved for our scrutiny, it has stood still.

Inscription on back: None
Era: c. 1950s–60s
Found in: USA

Cowgirls

The perfect pose. Mother and daughter gaze on cue, but while their smiles seem genuine, the kitten in this photo is where I get an insight into the real emotion at the heart of this photo. I can feel the thoughts in her eyes as she gazes down. Unlike the practised beauty queen poses of the humans, she is all natural, unaware of the scene being created around her – what is expected in a photo. Her paws, stretched out and a little clumsily large for her size, are just too fascinating. The world and this new body are more fascinating than the person with the camera. You cannot force a cat of any age to look at you.

Something in the development of the photo has distorted the carefully practised perfection: a paint smear of a processing accident creeps near and blurs the arm of the sofa and the mother's feet. I like to think the kitten conjured it, that there had to be a moment beyond their control to balance things out, to show the beauty of imperfection, the things that could be seen as mistakes.

The choice of all black in the girl's clothing though is a strange one – more Zorro than beauty pageant. And the sofa is so understated, so ordinary in its grey, when together the characters in this image are so extraordinary.

But within the pose the grin of the small girl in her cowgirl hat cannot be faked. She loves that kitten, possibly insisted on it being in the shot – *I will smile and sit perfectly still and wear the outfit, but the kitten must be in it too!* The kitten is her stripy, furry friend. She says more about how this small child wants to be seen than any hat could.

Inscription: Nov 10th 1931
Found in: USA

The Great Escape

November and bare legs, sundress, the USA's Deep South
I think, for this Indian summer of a day when the kittens
escaped. They just couldn't stay in the basket – not with all the
sun and the greenery and their energy just waiting to be spent.

Timmy is a blur, a high-speed superhero flash of a kitten, as
he leaps out and down for the great escape. Tommy is more
playful and easily distracted – he tumbles and stretches out
a paw to encourage his shyer brother Tibs, who peers out,
glowing as if radioactive. Do they all have their superhero
powers that they are using to avoid the woman capturing
them and bundling them back into the basket?

She looks poised for some kind of action, though catching
three superhero kittens is no easy task, especially if they're
working together.

She doesn't look mean, more frustrated or worn out, the
feeling any parent of toddlers would understand, but they are
taking no chances. This is their shot at freedom; their chance
to run and set up base and take over/save the world. Cats make
even better superheroes than humans. They are good at secret
identities, at keeping things hidden.

Nov 10 -1931

Inscription on back: None
Era: c. 1940s
Found in: Unknown

Julia and Moppet

Horizontal layers, pellucid light-smoke and an almost imperceptible carving of words. I am not even sure of the alphabet – too faint to sense Latin or Cyrillic. It's a curious thing with strangers' photographs, that without landmarks, apart from the tiniest of clues, visual guesses, it is hard to know which country they are in.

Moppet is preoccupied by the lonely shadow of a dinosaur in the bottom stripe of light – its long neck is all swan-like as Julia stares mid-word at the camera. Knees pulled in, bow draping like a strange padded harness to keep Moppet close to her. A galaxy of lichen watches her shoe. She holds Moppet still, knowing her tendency to run. She will join her soon – they will run through the streets together, trail sticks on railings, chase pigeons and shout at the sky. Her neatly parted hair, clips in place, hides her true wildness, how much she and Moppet share on these anonymous streets – the joy of all the freedom waiting for them when the taking of this image is over.

Inscription on back: None
Era: c. 1950s
Found in: USA

—

Jane and James

Sitting in the communal park by their flat they are all angles, the bench as if tilted; she leans to counterbalance it and stop them sliding off. James sits patiently. A little tired, paws draped over the edge – he's doing ever so well not to eat the rabbit she insists on placing on her lap to make this a true family portrait. The rabbit sits motionless, camouflaged through sheer will – accessory not prey is the plan, even though sometimes it's tempting to nibble the woven folds of Jane's skirt.

Jane has worn her best brooch for the occasion, more a corsage in scale and decorative ambition. It is all for the casual showing off – the pride in this moment in the city. They are happy and together; the grass full of squashed dandelions, daisies and sun.

The distant urban bustle beyond the park and flats, beyond the two-tiered verandas next to modern stone, is somewhere they will never walk all together: this is a moment to be still.

Inscription on back: None
Era: c. 1950s-60s
Found in: USA

—

Krypton Girl

She has not noticed the UFO ball of light, the sign from space, the portal to a different world. Tigger has. He is curling his tail away. Staring and stretching a paw to test the edges of what looks like a force field.

Her fringe is newly cut, a bow in her hair and white t-shirt still clean, despite the time of day. This is the only photo I've found taken out of doors when dark, and her cheeky grin suggests a victory in staying up late with her beloved kitten. *Look at us!*

Yet, there is something unearthly about the whole image, not just the strange light. She is peculiarly isolated here, a child in a bubble, landed from somewhere else. Childhood eighties films – *E.T.*, *Flight of the Navigator* . . . Magic child. Cat of Krypton. Landed in a field with the appearance of creatures we know, but somehow other, somehow special.

Inscription on back: None
Era: c. 1940s
Found in: France

The French
Wicker Throne

So proud. She is showcasing him. The old wicker chair, arms repaired differently and a plain cushion, should be a throne, carved and jewel studded, cushion of finest velvet with silk tassels. She grins as she rests her hands on him. *Just look at my pride and joy!* There will always be a record now.

The garden is alive with summer sun and trees brought to life after sleeping the winter away. Grass long and swaying, brushing ankles, just the right height for a miniature cat jungle full of unsuspecting shrews and mice. It has the atmosphere of a magical realm, an idyllic place of escape that should have a flower-strewn cottage nearby, with old beams and faded lace curtains, birds that talk back to you in the glinting evening light.

The garden is overgrown, but in a good way. His coat is long. Their love is not overgrown, but just right.

Inscription on back: Edith [seller's
writing so do not know if true name]
Era: c. 1940s
Found in: USA

-

A World Traveller

I know that this woman travelled the world and was maybe
called Edith. But her photos were left to a yard sale in Orange
County. Yet for all the adventure, this is a photo of home,
I think. Sitting on the steps, she seems to strike a home
posture, though she is held in – very upright and smart for a
day off from adventure . . . Her black dress is a formality of
neat shoulders, with a dark picket fence of trimming, a single
centred brooch and the smudges of shadows.

She looks at him, holds out a stick with a thin thread to
tease him softly towards her. He, on tip toes, watches the dark
line where her calves press together, knees the top, ankles the
bottom of a heart. The gate is a star, all wood, like the house.
Strange he thinks, what things were once trees. He is unsure
of his approach.

His whiskers smudge the air – a curious overgrowing, more
than is needed to enable him to squeeze through gaps, to check
he'll fit through hidden doors. He is a skinny sweet thing.

There is a corner of light fingers, near the steps, a smeared alien handprint. Another on her knee – it glows.

He tentatively moves higher. Where has she been all this time? He did not see her on his street patrol. Something smells different, now she's back with him. She is having to gain his trust again, not get lost in the memories of her travels.

She stays still as the string on the stick trembles.

Inscription on back: For Gracie. Gracie and
the wealthy [indecipherable] and the kittens.
Era: c. 1950s
Found in: USA

-

For Gracie

Only one is named. *For Gracie. Gracie and the wealthy* [name as sqiggle] *and the kittens.* With their matching floral swirls of suits, this name loss somehow blends the girls together. The curse and joy of being a twin – the inescapable blurring of identity. They could both be Gracie, or neither.

One girl is smiling, one unsure. There is one hair bow – a butterfly aircraft alighting – and one grown-out fringe side parted to help tell them apart. Then there are the kittens: one rising, another lying still; one white, one tabby – different personalities shown not so much in their colour as how they sit in the girls' laps.

I wonder how they chose their feline friends. If both wanted the same kitten, or each has their true cat love. Did their parents give them distinctly different cats to help tell them apart, which they could not bear to do with outfits? Or were they chosen? Cats do such things. Are they clues to the girls' real personalities? They saw the differences others could not – that these girls do not match despite their attire, despite the faces they couldn't change. They are unique. The kittens love them as they truly are – different to each other.

Inscription on back: None
Era: c. 1900s
Found in: UK

The Secret Cat
on a Hat

Two speckles of light hover on her hair as if they are the
eyes of another smaller black cat sitting on her head – the
latest accessory – an almost invisible, peculiarly camouflaged
miniature cat hat to be friends with the other that merges into
her dress as it sits on her lap. This cat is somewhat grander and
gazes more at ease than her owner who is strangely still, arms
obscured at her sides, buckled feet neatly turned out.

I feel like half of this photo is missing; something or someone
was cut out. White dress, white cat, white deck chair – was
someone else next to her too bright and patterned? A joyous
clash or someone she'd rather forget; a memory easier lost than
constantly reviewed?

Or was it just the perfection of this portrait that made
her want to tear the rest of it away – the strangeness of the
colour scheme and pose, the secret cat hat, the black beads
a magical collar, the burst of spell light at the bottom, the
subtle drapery of leaves?

Inscription on back: None
Era: c. 1960s
Found in: USA

Three Girls,
Morning Surprise

Kneel down and pray to the cult of the cat in a box.

Three ages, three smiles, three fringes. Outfits that suggest a strange commonality – not quite a uniform, not something worn to school, so much as a code, an outfit for their secret club of cat-in-box worshippers.

They are waiting for something special. For the object of their delight to emerge, but this rebirth from a box to a new place might as well be a portal as far as the cat is concerned. One home, then darkness and rustled noises, then another home. She had not walked anywhere. What is this strange magic?

The fireplace feels as if stretched to the ceiling, in a house where the scale is all wrong. A fairy-tale shrinkage that led to a closed box, opened reverently. A cat in a box, back leg springs, a discarded bow to hunt later.

She is not sure what to do next – with all these eyes upon her, the speckled carpet floor, the lack of furniture. Is the only territory that is hers this box? Their hands are not reaching for strokes yet, still glued together in praise of instructions. Then, camera stilled, she ventures into their world.

Inscription on back: None
Era: c. 1920s–40s
Found in: UK

-

Inside Out

Strange to be held with such lack of support – legs and tail hanging, body a strange fluffy twist in contrast to a furry face that is almost content. Wistful maybe. She knows that her owner wants to show off all her softness – a nod to the gentle against the harsh black of her sensible suit.

There is a smoky oil slick of dark from her feet, spilling over the lawn. It takes flowers in its stride – snuffs them out. I think of The Groke in the *Moomins* – how she unintentionally steals the light. I always felt she was misunderstood and I wonder if this woman is in her dark attire. She might have reached an age where colour was seen as inappropriate, or be mourning, or perhaps she has a sensible job where frills would not be tolerated.

Her garden is beautiful and full of sun. Her cat is white and all candyfloss, despite the strange grip she has on her. If this woman was dark the cat would have fled. She is letting herself be put on display: an embodiment of the inside of her owner. Appearances can be deceiving. Together, the dark and the light, they make the perfect pair in this English cottage garden.

Inscription on backs: None
Era: c. 1910s
Found in: Germany

A Tale of Two Blossoms

Light as dark, dark as light. The sisters take turns to sit
with him. Same tree. Once all white, once a division, a sepia
stripe of ragged light, purpling half the petals. Same fence
or building with vertical plank eyes. Same patch of grass.
Same cat. Yet there are two stories.

Light: The light hides a little darkness. Solemn stare, she
holds him tight – protectively. It is a fierce love: he has to love
her best, just has to . . . She wills it.

Plaits wrap round her head to hold her craziest crown
– the tree is growing from her, an extravagance of blossom
fanning a peacock's tail. Perhaps her frown is concentration
not ill humour – the tricky balance of such a dryadesque
accessory while holding on to a young cat who has evidently
seen something worth investigating.

White frilled cardigan, cream blouse and checked skirt, an apron for him to sit on. It would be a fairly practical outfit were it not for the tree.

I wonder what happens next. As her tree crown turns summer its blossom turns to leaves, which leave her come autumn, just as he does as soon as this photo is over and he runs at the petals dancing in breezes like little pink tongues.

Waiting can be painful. Especially for wanted change – oh how she longs for change. But whatever may happen, he will return come teatime.

Dark: A gentler, rounder face and posture, slight slouch as he sits on her knee, paws held softly, he is not making a run for it here. Black dress, sombre despite the lace collar, folded-in wings perhaps, but this dark picture holds more light.

He feels both delight and safety with her, a companionship, less fierce than her sister's love. The tree is just a tree here, though no less beautiful and split in hues – and it is on the darker side she sits, the bright side left empty as if missing her sister, who is not really dark, but too bright for this world and such brightness can burst and be too much.

He loves them both though. A tale of two halves.

The birds watch on and whisper.

Bibliography and Further Reading

The introductory essay is greatly indebted to the wonderful facts and information in the following books:

Burroughs, William S., *The Cat Inside*, Penguin Modern Classics, 2009 (first published 1992)

Chaucer, Geoffrey, trans. Coghill, Nevill (1951), *The Canterbury Tales*, Penguin Classics, 2003

Chitty, Susan, *Gwen John 1876-1939*, Hodder and Stoughton, 1986 (first published 1981)

Donovan, Frank, *Never on a Broom Stick*, Allen & Unwin Ltd, 1973

Hole, Christina, *Witchcraft in England*, Book Club Associates by arrangement with B. T. Batsford Ltd, 1977

Hole, Christina, *English Folklore*, B. T. Batsford Ltd, 1940

Oldall Addy, Sidney, *Folk Tales and Superstitions*, EP Publishing Ltd, 1973 (first published 1895)

Sontag, Susan, *On Photography*, Penguin Modern Classics, 2008 (first published 1977)

Thomas, Keith, *Man and the Natural World: Changing Attitudes in England 1500-1800*, Penguin, 1984

Walker-Meikle, Kathleen, *Cats in Medieval Manuscripts*, The British Library, 2011 and 2019

Wright, Michael and Walters, Sally, eds, *The Book of the Cat*, Pan Books, 1980

Acknowledgements

I would like to thank the brilliant women in my life and dear friends.

Chandra Haabjoern, Emily Hammond, Ana Seferovic, Alice Stevenson, Astrid Johnston, Hannah Little, Maka Bubashvili, Jodi Auld, Natalija Simovic, Teo Natsvlishvili, Sue Bishop and Nicola Harding. For reading endless past work, Amber Hitchman and Sara Veal. For brilliant pointers on portraits of women and cats, Bryony Coombes, and excellent esoteric suggestions, Emily Bick (I wish I could have fitted more in).

I would also like to thank the fantastic members of the Bath Festivals Young Writers Lab who I have had the privilege to teach. Travis Elborough for always supporting my writing. Kamila Galczynska for being the best vet ever. Sam Roberts for rescuing so many cats, including Tariel and Sindri. Everyone at September for supporting this book and understanding it from the start. And lastly Dylan's previous owners for letting me have him – it meant the world.

About the Author

Alice Maddicott is a writer and artist from Somerset, England. Her work has spanned poetry, writing installations, children's television scripts (*The Large Family, The Clangers*), travel and nature writing, including for *Elsewhere Journal* and the *Waymaking* anthology, as well as public art commissions such as *The Car Boot Museum*. For nearly two decades she has worked on creative education projects and run writing workshops with young people. She lives with two rescue cats, Tariel and Sindri, and Ptolemy the tortoise who she's had for 35 years.

Alice and Dylan, 2011.